Journeying Out

Journeying Out

A New Approach to Christian Mission

Ann Morisy

MOREHOUSE PUBLISHING
A Continuum imprint
www.morehousepublishing.com

Morehouse
Continuum imprint
The Tower Building
11 York Road
London SE1 7NX

15 East 26th Street
New York
NY 10010

www.continuumbooks.com

First published 2004

British Library Cataloguing-in-Publication Data
A catalogue record for this book is available from the British Library.

ISBN 978 0 8192 8101 2

Typeset by YHT Ltd, London
Printed and bound by Biddles Ltd, King's Lynn, Norfolk

Contents

Acknowledgements

I should like to thank a number of people who have helped me with this book: Simon Grigg, Judith Daley and Dorothy Stewart-Courtis for their helpful comments on clumsy early drafts; Sue Cope for definitive and welcome guidance on the final manuscript; Caroll Potter for her generous practical help; Susie Paddock for much encouragement and to Margaret Kesterton who did all three. To everyone involved in the process I express warm thanks and deep appreciation.

Introduction

The inspiration for this book comes from David Bosch who coined the term holistic mission. Bosch, using impressive scholarship, traced how the idea and practice of mission has changed and developed throughout the history of the Church.[1] The very fact that our understanding has changed over time, Bosch suggests, should encourage us today to experiment and investigate new approaches to mission. We shouldn't be hobbled by the idea of a purist model of mission that is 'God given'. However, Bosch speculates that mission, at its best, contributes both to the Kingdom of God and to the awakening of faith, and that for holistic mission neither is prior to the other. Tragically, David Bosch died in a road accident in his native South Africa, so we are unable to quiz him about this perception of how the domains of social action and evangelism could be integrated in a way that is viable in our peculiar post-modern context.

I write with some urgency. I am aware that many of the community ministry projects that churches have set up are increasingly being viewed as expendable. As financial pressures start to mount within the established denominations the pressure to use the church hall to maximize income rather than for the sidelined and struggling means that the Church's community care can get short shrift. Likewise the pressure, especially on clergy, to play an active part in *neighbourhood renewal* initiatives brings confused agendas and the potential for mission gains associated with community involvement to be relegated in favour of influencing decision-makers. An assessment of the Church's community involvement is needed before it is too late. This book is a contribution to that assessment. However, it is not just an evaluation of community ministry that is presented here, it is a commendation. A strong case is made for there being a host of unacknowledged beneficial outcomes associated with community ministry. Furthermore, journeying out to encounter those who know deeply about struggle is the route by which we experience the extraordinarily grace-full outcome of holistic mission.

The most concise way of providing an overview of my argument is to list the ten propositions that together summarize the thesis of this book.

Ten propositions

Proposition one

Increasingly churches are running social projects. This might seem an excellent development, but we need to be careful that we don't allow the idea of 'needs meeting' to dominate our thinking. 'Needs meeting' as an organizing principle for the Church's social action fails to do justice to the radical and very practical teaching and example of Jesus.

Proposition two

In the complex world in which we live it is sometimes necessary to pursue one's objective obliquely. From some perspectives an oblique approach can appear as ill-disguised trickery, whilst from another, as a wise and welcome intuitive approach. Perhaps it is both of these things. This principle of obliquity would seem to be important if we are to achieve *holistic* mission.

Proposition three

All of us, especially those of us living in suburbia, crave a story-rich life. The process of achieving a story-rich life often involves us taking the risk of being overwhelmed.

Proposition four

Truth is tricky. We have to take more seriously how prone we are to deluding ourselves that we have the truth. Furthermore, the scope for delusion is greatest when we are powerful – and when we are anxious, and may God help us when the powerful are also anxious. Truth is relational, in other words our journey towards truth relies on encounter with others – especially an encounter with those who are different from us.

Proposition five

All of us have an urge to experience transformation and to move closer to a better self. One important aspect of this urge to be a better person is to become a more moral person.

Proposition six

Religious experience is alive and well and often triggered by the possibility of being overwhelmed. Along with the principal of obliquity the phenomenon of religious experience is important if we are to achieve *holistic* mission.

Proposition seven

Throughout history, most of the Christian faithful have been captivated by rulers and empires. It is only as churches have been stripped of power that we have begun to get the gist of the Gospel. The vulnerability that we experience today presents us with glorious new possibilities.

Proposition eight

We must be as confident in the reality of virtuous circles as we are troubled by the reality of vicious circles. In other words do we have confidence in the great cascades of grace that enfold us when we are in the right place?

Proposition nine

The right place is when, without power and at risk of being overwhelmed, we are prepared to embrace struggle on behalf of others.

Proposition ten

The invitation to call God our Father brings with it the blessing of fraternal relations with all God's children. This is the basis of Jesus' practice of boundary-breaking compassion, which the Church is called to emulate.[2]

This book has been written in such a way that each of the first six chapters and Chapter 9 can stand alone. However, the themes that are considered in these chapters are pulled together in the final three chapters in which a model of holistic mission is proposed that is made up of three domains: the explicit, the foundational and the vocational.

I have made a point of spelling out what each bit of jargon means when I first use it. However, if it crops up again at a later point in the book it is possible to check it out in the glossary. Please do not be put off by what may seem to be a lot of jargon; the technical expressions I use are just building blocks for my argument that I have drawn from a number of disciplines. Please enjoy the end of chapter notes, often they are asides that I have been unable to resist – and am probably unable to justify!

Notes

1 Throughout this book I use 'The Church' as a fully inclusive term, implying all denominations, new churches, the established Church, pastors and people.

2 David Bosch, *Transforming Mission*, (New York: Orbis, 1991), p. 86.

1

Entering an Adaptive Zone

I was asked to meet some Russians visiting Britain. (Their aim was to learn from the English churches how in post Soviet Russia the churches could contribute to community well-being.) I began straightforwardly enough - or so I thought. I told them I was employed by the Diocese of London and that the Diocese was founded in 604 AD. The interpreter came to a halt almost immediately. 'Had I really said 604? Did I mean to say 604?' she queried. I confirmed the date only to witness the confusion spread among the wider group. The Russian visitors shook their heads and debated between them - Could I really have said that the Diocese went back so far? Had the interpreter made a mistake? They were right to look askance. It is rare to come across an organisation that can trace its roots back 300 years and to find one that goes back well over 1,000 years is quite extraordinary. And there we have it. The Church's longevity is quite extraordinary.

Whilst it is common to hear moans about how resistant the Church is to change, such criticism may be misplaced. The Church is incredibly resilient to have weathered the storms for two millennia. Surely, nothing the Church has to face today can match the traumas of the repeated reformations the Church faced in England in the sixteenth and seventeenth centuries. Even during the twentieth century, the Church of England changed beyond recognition as it escaped the cultural control of the powerful in the land. The changes that came as a result of clergy encountering the hardships of men living and dying in the trenches during the First World War prompted the early fissures in the established way of being church and its embodiment in the role of clergyman.

It is easy to miss the occasions that have prompted change within the Church. This is especially the case today when the steady decline in Church membership and attendance dominates our perceptions. It is tempting to think that we face some awful end game. However history makes clear that this sense of vulnerability and possible demise has been a recurring experience. Nevertheless, it would be irresponsible to be casual in the face of a crisis simply because the Church has a track record of being able to weather a storm, but it should give us confidence that we are part of an enterprise that is responsive and adaptable.

Given the extraordinary longevity of our churches it is worth considering some of the insights available from the world of biology. Biology is one of the few disciplines which takes seriously the dimension of time. Although the evolutionary journey of a species is profoundly longer than the life history of the Church, there may be something we can learn from biologists in their study of evolution. For example, in their concern for evolutionary processes biologists recognize critical moments in the development of a species. Species sometimes enter into a distinct 'adaptive zone' when there is a leap in the development of the organism in response to its environment. Biologists are also clear that a species is only effective in its evolutionary journey if it engages with, or rubs up against, the challenges presented by the wider environment. All species and organisms have to actively and continually engage with their external environment in order to ensure longevity and productivity. Management consultants give the same message to organizations. The challenge of *journeying out* and rising above the discomfort associated with this kind of risk-taking is essential to the long-term survival of our corporate enterprises as well as for God's creatures.

For the Church today the challenge is to find a way of focusing our attention *outside* the institution and to resist the temptation to become preoccupied with the insistent, internal demands for more money, new roofs, more clergy, more children in the Sunday School and more young families in the pews. However, the insistent demands of the institution, both at denominational and local level, are only part of the story. Journeying out requires the capacity to rise above the anxiety associated with encountering and embracing a potentially overwhelming, outside world.

Over the last twenty years there have been commendable examples of churches making the effort to *journey out*. An early impetus for this was the policies pursued by the Thatcher Government during the 1980s. Leaving aside the long-term rights and wrongs of Conservative social policies during this period, what is indisputable is that the tough social policies brought about evident poverty throughout Britain. Whilst some people undoubtedly flourished during this period, the visibility of the poor increased and respectable Britain was confronted by people sleeping on the street, in shop doorways or in bus stations. Peeked, drawn faces of children became more visible and hypothermia among elderly people made the news. Prior to this, church-going, respectable Britain had been protected from the needs of the poor by a functioning welfare state.

Virtually all the mainstream denominations in Britain produced reports[1] which protested at the state of the nation and how the burden of change was falling disproportionately on poor communities. Britain in the 1980s, with the dismantling of welfare provision, had become a different environment for the churches and for people of faith, and therefore it demanded a different response. Church members could no longer live with the guilt of passing by unconcerned when confronted by people and communities where poverty and distress was so visible. Churches, both locally and nationally, began to respond and mobilize effort on behalf of poor people. Spurred on by the parable of the Good Samaritan[2] this

3

produced an *adaptive zone* for the Church, offering a leap in the development of our way of being church in response to the wider environment.

During the 1980s and for much of the 1990s the traditional voluntary and community sector was very fragile as its grant aid from cash-strapped local authorities evaporated. This meant that churches often found themselves as the sole survivors in areas of multiple deprivation, and despite facing their own pressures to remain viable often courageously took steps to initiate a community project. Funding from the Church Urban Fund, established by the Church of England but available to any faith community with a project in an 'urban priority area', gave energy to these local or neighbourhood initiatives. The repertoire of the clergy widened to encompass the skills of project design and management, and they invested time in networking – alongside their traditional commitment to visit the sick and the dying.

The emergence of holistic mission

At the same time as churches were becoming more inclined towards social action, David Bosch's book *Transforming Mission*[3] began to attract attention. Bosch's seminal work legitimized social engagement as a purposeful expression of mission. Bosch demonstrated how *mission* had been understood in different ways throughout the history of the Church. On the basis of this rigorous analysis Bosch began to articulate a *holistic* view of mission that included social action as an essential component of mission. Bosch challenged the usual understanding of purposeful mission, i.e. the proclamation of and encouragement of people to acknowledge the salvation brought by Jesus. He observed that the Church in the West had become preoccupied with personal salvation, and undervalued the actions and teaching that Jesus demonstrated in his daily life. We are too inclined to read the Gospels as 'Passion histories with extensive introductions' (here Bosch is quoting Kähler[4]), to the extent that, for the Western Church, the essence of the Gospel has become 'Christ died for my sins on the cross'.

This reading of the Gospel, Bosch suggests, has inclined churches to consider proclamatory evangelism as their primary task. With social justice tending to be viewed as a *fruit* of people turning to Christ, i.e. the successful proclamation of salvation causes or prompts a movement towards social justice. According to Bosch this sequential view of mission fails to do justice to the fact that Jesus *both* inaugurated salvation *and* provided us with a model of life to emulate. It is this integration of Christ's life with His death and resurrection that is the basis of Bosch's 'holistic mission'.

In *Transforming Mission* Bosch also emphasized how the Church's life and work are intimately bound up with God's cosmic-historical plan for the salvation of the world. This requires Christians to see and understand themselves as kingdom people, not church people. We must not fall into the temptation of treating the Church, and faith itself, as 'a waiting room for the hereafter'. Bosch articulated clearly how 'the Church can only be a credible sacrament of salvation for the world when it displays to humanity a glimmer of God's imminent reign – a kingdom of reconciliation, peace and new life'.[5] With meticulous scholarship, Bosch demonstrated that mission which serves the Gospel has to manifest itself in action, and not just in the proclamation of a message of salvation in the world to come. The Church, if it is to honour the Gospel, has to journey out, embrace strangers, work for social peace and justice and partake of God's gracious gift of salvation.

The availability and exceptional calibre of Bosch's work was timely, for it provided a theological context for the many local expressions of social action that occurred in Britain from 1985 onwards. Thanks to Bosch the status of social action as an essential, non-negotiable part of mission has begun to be acknowledged. Community involvement and social action in the pursuit of justice has become a legitimate objective for the Church alongside helping people to discover a living faith in Christ.[6] With this new perspective of holistic mission, no longer would a community project set up by a local church be dismissed as a return to a discredited 'social gospel'.[7] Now only the theologically uninformed and missiologically ignorant would, in the post-Bosch era, challenge the minister for acting like a social worker rather than a minister of the cloth or suggest that in practising social action one risked turning the Church into a social-work agency.[8]

There is another factor that has given social action a fair wind. Intuitively, it was recognized that the great evangelistic rallies, characterized by Billy Graham and others, could no longer have the same impact as they had in the 1950s and 60s. The prevalence of rival ways of making sense of the world now made it impossible for anyone to tell or urge upon another what to believe. The rival *plausibility structures*, or world views, that confronted 'Joe Public' meant that embracing a faith would be a personal and idiosyncratic journey. In this context, authenticity has become the looked for characteristic and pointer to what is believable. Words and actions have to be in step if one is to earn the right to be listened to. *Walking the talk* has become an essential aspect of evangelism, and therefore community involvement can no longer be treated as an option; rather it has become an essential tactic if a platform for mission (i.e. proclamation) is to be created in a post-modern and post-Christendom context. However, such *tactical* use of social action falls far short of Bosch's understanding of holistic mission. Using social action as a means to an end must not be allowed to pass as a full-bodied expression of holistic mission. Not least because in struggling with the challenge of how to link what Jesus did in His life with what He achieved through His death and resurrection we may discover that the ways in which Jesus worked and the processes that He adopted are both significant and practical.

Jesus, in His life, as Bosch insistently reminds the Western Church, gave many insights and directions and urged us to emulate His actions. We know what we have to do: to eschew power as it is used by the mainstream, and to stand alongside the poor. These clear practices of Jesus, have, during the millennium in which the Church has wielded power, been masked by our preoccupation with the far more accommodating, but false, summary of Jesus' teaching, as 'Love the Lord your God with all your heart and all your soul and love other people as yourself'.[9] In reciting this summary of the Law, Jesus was demonstrating his knowledge of Jewish teaching. He was not proffering it as His mission statement. Jesus' teaching and actions would not have sat quite so comfortably with the Church's historic inclination to shore up the rich and the powerful.

The new environment to which the Church has to adapt is characterized more by our powerlessness than by our power. This loss of power and influence by churches enables us to move closer to the poor, and with this, our understanding of the Gospel has been transformed. By standing alongside the poor we begin to see and understand that the poor and oppressed may indeed have a mysterious part in the purposes of God and Jesus' suggestion that the first shall be last and the last shall be first seems less of a teasing conundrum or naive optimism verging on fable. Experience of being alongside the poor and discounted, at a minimum, scrambles stereotypes, and, at its best, enables the Church to understand what it is that Jesus was going on about. And this gives hope that the genuine practicality, as well as the reality, of the upside-down values and processes that Jesus commended will enter the Church's bloodstream. In God's generous economy, *whenever* we do what is right (and often despite questionable motivation) a cascade of grace is likely to follow. And knowing what is right is easier than we are often prepared to acknowledge.

Experiencing the radically different order that Jesus promises

Whilst only the learned might grapple with Bosch's treatise, an encounter with the poor via the myriad church projects that have been set up has triggered a profound theological shift within the Church – at all levels. Experiences and Gospel insight have started to feed into each other. We have begun to recognize that the actions and teaching of Jesus are radically different from even the most benign social practices that prevail in our world. It is impossible to overemphasize the shaking of the foundations that has been set in train by this dawning awareness. Our capacity to distinguish Gospel values from worthy, worldly values has been enhanced. Furthermore, a seed has been sown which brings a new humility to the Church. We can now *see* our Church structures as repeatedly mirroring the ways of the world. Now we can accept (and even cherish!), the enduring fact of our corporate 'feet of clay', because we have begun to see that our work has to be for the sake of the Gospel and not for the sake of the Church. In our new post-Christendom environment we can now see the extent of our delusions, and it makes for humility and a renewed awareness of our need for God. When we start to see things differently we also see new priorities.

The lesson we have learnt over the last twenty years is that obedience to Jesus begins in relation to the poor and marginalized. This lesson has always been there for us to learn. However, in the West we have proved to be rather slow learners. Jim Wallis of the Sojourner Community provides a neat illustration of this. The Sojourner Community in downtown Washington rattled the cages of the respectable churches in the City and challenged them to express a commitment to the poor. Their hearers often tried to deflect the challenge by questioning the Community's interpretation of the Bible. Surely the Bible does not give such a clear mandate to be alongside those who are vulnerable and oppressed? Jim Wallis, in response to such quarrelsome reactions, responded by taking scissors to his Bible and cut out every reference to 'the poor'. For many years Jim Wallis used the resulting 'fallen apart' Bible to illustrate his case.

A more studied response to the non-negotiable call to attend to the needs of the poor is provided by Conrad Boerma in his book *Rich Man, Poor Man and the Bible*.[10] Here Boerma tracks the relationship between the rich and the poor during the different stages of the history of the Children of Israel. He notes that in the early, patriarchal society described in the first five books of the Bible, poverty is not an issue.[11] Later, with the settlement of land and the development of a monarchy the distinction between rich and poor starts to emerge, with examples such as Solomon instigating forced labour to build the Temple (1 Kings 5.13 and also 1 Kings 15.22).[12] Archeologists also provide evidence of a separation between rich and poor. Boerma notes that the excavations at Tirzah show that in the tenth century BC housing is of an equal size and quality. Only two hundred years later there is a clear contrast between the housing for the wealthy and the slums for the poor.[13] The Prophets emerge in the eighth century BC to protest that the rich are the cause of the poverty and that the growing distress of the poor indicates that the rich have turned their backs on God.

The Bible, therefore, does not give a straightforward message. Boerma notes that books such as Proverbs and Ecclesiastes, which emanate from courtly circles, provide a different perspective on the poor and the rich. These books of the wisdom tradition speak of an acceptance of a stratified society, with the poor being despised for their deficiency. The perspective emerges that if riches are a blessing then poverty must be a curse. Therefore poverty carries an additional burden: no longer is poverty just about a lack of material resources, it also carries the stigma of shame and guilt.

Boerma, in turning to the Gospels, comments that they teem with references to the rich and the poor and with various Greek words used to articulate different emphases. In particular, Boerma notes the distinction between *ptóchos*, referring to the man who is reduced to begging and not respectable, and *penés* implying a man, who despite his poverty, endeavours to live frugally and respectably.[14] Here we have echoes of the distinction between the deserving and undeserving poor that preoccupies students of social policy today. Increasingly our social policies have settled into practices that try to take account of the needs of the respectable poor, whereas the wilful or uncooperative poor receive short shrift or are even punished. However, within the Gospels we find a different emphasis. For Jesus, in teaching 'blessed are the poor', uses the word *ptóchos*. Blessed are the undeserving, i.e. those who are not respectable.

Such statements of Jesus, even when part of the famous Beatitudes, are often looked upon sceptically, as being so heavenly minded that they can be of no earthly use. Surely Jesus' comments must belong to the world to come, not this world ... surely they cannot be a practical teaching that can inform our daily practice? Surely this gracious economy in which Jesus urges us to participate cannot add up? Remarkably, over the last twenty years the 'needs must' indignation (and guilt) provoked in churches by abrasive Thatcherism has meant that churches have opened their doors (at least the doors of their church halls) to the *ptóchos*, the far from respectable poor. The adaptive zone that we have entered has given us a remarkable opportunity to test the practicality of Jesus' radical teaching.

Of course, just as God has his own distinct economy so too does Old Nick. Alongside this major leap of understanding and insight comes the noisy anxiety associated with trying to maintain our habitual way of being church when the costs of trying to do so have rocketed. Our inclination to disregard God's gracious economy and opt for worldly ways is fed by anxiety. When anxiety is in the air we fight to resist change and our confidence in journeying out and engaging with this new, adaptive zone evaporates. Anxiety turns us inwards and drains us of energy, so we get preoccupied with more and more analysis and dare only to tweak our structures, rather than turn outwards to practise Gospel obedience in our neighbourhoods and world. Furthermore, in concentrating on the needs of the Church we will find ourselves bringing further decline upon ourselves. It is not just for the sake of the

Gospel that we have to rise above this anxiety,[15] it is also for the sake of the Church. We have to decide whether or not we trust Jesus' teaching and practice of solidarity with the *ptóchos*, the undeserving, and we have to decide whether we trust the dynamics at the heart of God's gracious economy that when we struggle for righteousness in relation to Jesus' teaching and practice we will find ourselves being 'church'.

When we find our obedience to the Gospel in our local context God's blessings may both surprise and subvert the accepted ways of the world. There are real-world examples of this. The winter night shelters that run in a number of locations in London provide an illustration of the very graceful outcomes that seem to come when we can put anxiety aside and embrace an outward orientation. The example I use also illustrates *the principle of obliquity* which I believe is essential to the full expression of holistic mission.

In many of the inner boroughs of London there have been more and more homeless people living on the street.[16] An initiative began among the churches in the borough of Newham. Seven churches each took it in turn to open their church hall for the evening and through the night to provide shelter during the winter months. Between them they could ensure seven-day-a-week provision. The following year the churches in Hackney made similar provision, and were followed the next year by churches in Islington and West London who developed their own schemes. A momentum has developed and churches have been quick to learn from each other.

It is the Hackney story that I share but similar experiences could be logged in each of the schemes. Hackney is one of the poorest boroughs in London. The churches for the most part are short of resources (just like the borough). Perhaps this was one of the reasons why the venture happened at all. Many of the church halls were decrepit and perhaps this helped churches to agree to their use, for who else but the homeless on a bitterly cold night would be happy to make use of such a woebegone hall?

Two women carried the story of what the churches had done in Newham, and posed the straightforward question

'Can't we do something like this in Hackney?' The more 'successful' churches had the option of sloping off, avoiding the challenge. Their high-quality halls were likely to be in full use, Brownie packs and badminton clubs filling every available evening and the playgroup or Mums and Toddlers needing the facilities first thing each morning. Those churches whose halls were close to tumbling down had no such excuse. Their halls were more or less empty. They were the ones who faced a sharper debate about involvement in the scheme.

The challenge to get involved meant that anxiety had to be faced about a number of issues: the genuine fear of those who were on the streets – alcoholics, drug addicts, people with uncontrolled mental illness, people with TB or AIDS, people with fleas or hair lice. ... The list of possible threats was endless. To say 'yes' to involvement meant finding a way through this thicket of worry. The alternative was to slip into an anxious neurosis which could only recite the reasons for walking away from the challenge. A second source of anxiety was the amount of organisation and teamwork that would be needed. There was no track record of collaboration to give confidence that people would pull together to cover all the tasks.

The factor which helped churches to rise above their anxieties was that overall it was only for three months – just twelve sessions for each of the seven participating churches. Furthermore other churches in similar straitened circumstances seemed to have been able to cope and there was a promise of volunteers from other churches to help plug gaps in the rota. Throughout all the debate (and the debate had to be conducted at a pace because winter was getting closer) there was a mixture of guilt associated with refusing to get involved, and a sense that to say 'yes' was to do the right thing. After the pros and cons had been weighed, the wise maxim 'when you don't know what to do, do what Jesus would do' tipped the balance away from an anxious 'no' towards a positive 'yes'.

In order to open the doors of the church hall for just one evening and through the night, a whole network of helpers had to be lined up; far more than could be assembled from a worn-down congregation. The little team that took on the challenge in each of the participating churches had to recruit their friends and neighbours and neighbours' friends to do all that needed to be done.

Each evening the hall was open a team would be needed in the kitchen as well as welcoming people and clearing tables. Another team would take responsibility for getting the camp beds out helped by those who would be sleeping on them. There would also be a sleepover team and an early morning team to cook breakfast and clear everything away until the following week. But that is only half of it.

Behind the scenes were people such as those who would pop their newspaper through Betty's letterbox so she could take it with her to the hall for the homeless people to read. There were others who each week made meat balls and a large apple crumble in readiness for the supper that would be served to far more than those who slept overnight. Others faithfully washed and ironed the sheets and towels. The battered church halls might not look much but the bed linen was always freshly laundered.

The fact that so many people were desperate enough to bed down in a church hall in the back streets of Hackney came as a shock. The group who held the venture together had never expected such a high level of need. They found themselves more and more indignant that their basic and amateur provision was so urgently needed. That indignation translated into an invitation to the Member of Parliament to come to a meeting to discuss homelessness in Hackney.

Bosch urges us to work for a closer interrelationship between social action and enabling people to embrace the Christian faith. Whilst intellectually we might assent to this it is more difficult to translate into action. Almost without exception our efforts to integrate work for justice with the recognition of Christ's unique saving power seems to drift into a sequential or consecutive process, with either social action or evangelism being treated as prior to the other. Could it be that activities such as the Hackney Churches Winter Nightshelter provide an oblique means of enabling people to embrace faith in Jesus as Saviour as well as contribute to the Kingdom of God? Might it be that in a complex, multifaith, multicultural, fragmented society the way to enable people to hear and cherish the Gospel is by way of an oblique route? And by way of this obliquity, which begins with solidarity with the poor, we might discover the means by which we are both *being* church, and *doing* mission.

This business of obliquity

The issue of obliquity, and its potential for enabling people to allow faith to unfurl within them, is supported by the insights of Michael Polanyi.[17] Polanyi is famed for his observation that *we can and do know more than we can tell*. In brief, Polanyi believed that we have defined knowledge far too narrowly, and this has led us to overlook the deep layer of knowledge that we cannot articulate in words. In particular, he suggests that there is a distinction between tacit knowing and explicit knowing. He writes, 'Generally speaking, we come to know the rich and more universal or comprehensive dimensions of our common experience by focusing on or attending to their meaning from or through the less complex particulars of which they are composed.'[18] In other words, we participate in more than a single aspect of experience at the same time but our awareness is only of a single aspect at any one time.

An immediate example of this is that in your efforts to make sense of what is being said here you will be relying on the regularity and consistency of the printed letters on this page and the rules of grammar. However, to focus on this level would cause you to lose or disrupt your ability to make sense of what is written. The fact that we can read 'automatically' is an example of the tacit knowledge that most people possess, but to bring that skill into consciousness would ruin its capacity to aid the transfer of ideas and enable communication. Polanyi would label the capacity to make sense of letters and grammar consistently as a *subsidiary awareness*, in that it is an experience which has to be taken for granted, i.e.

allowed to remain 'tacit' if it is to do its job. However, if this subsidiary awareness is brought into *focal awareness* it ceases to deliver, it ceases to work.

When tacit knowledge is focused upon it loses its capacity to be a medium through which meaning or a skill can be delivered. It is no longer able to carry the richer message or capacity. What Polanyi is getting at is that the richer comprehensions of our lives are mediated through lesser dimensions, without being explainable in terms of them. Much of the language that we use about faith clearly belongs to a tacit dimension. For example, to *know God* and to *love God* are what we crave but to focus on these capacities directly reduces them to more routine component parts, which somehow cannot be restacked in a way that equates to the state of loving and knowing God. Loving God and knowing God, if we *focus* on them get reduced to other levels such as prayerfulness, reflection on Scripture and acting in ways that we have come to understand as loving and compassionate. These things are valuable and desirable in themselves, but loving and knowing God are more than these things. This is what Polanyi is referring to when he suggests *we can and do know more than we can tell.*

Polanyi warns that in complex situations it is possible to mistake subsidiary (tacit) awareness for focal awareness. This warning raises the possibility that we have fallen into this confusion in relation to mission. Could it be that we treat mission as focal awareness when in fact it is something which needs to remain tacit? Is there a danger that when mission becomes a self-conscious phenomenon it ceases to deliver its intended objective? By *focusing* on mission local churches bring into conscious attention what might best remain 'tacit' or under the surface.[19]

There is a very down-to-earth parallel to this distinction between subsidiary and focal awareness and it is to be found in the business world. John Kay observes that to tell business managers 'Go and make money' provides very little guidance. The same instruction could be given to every business manager, whether working for Shell, Siemens or the Disney Corporation, for all of them have this same, tacit objective. The art of business leadership is to identify the distinctive route by which to achieve this tacit objective of significant profit. So for example, Disney employees are not told to go and make money for Disney, they are told 'To make sure the guests have fun'.[20] What is more, if the task of making money becomes a *focal* awareness, it works against that very outcome. In Polanyi's terms, making money has to remain a subsidiary awareness if the goal is to be achieved. So, the mission statements used by businesses and other commercial ventures articulate their distinctive focal awareness. They do not say that their business is to maximize profit, this purpose remains implicit or tacit. Kay refers to George Merck, the founder of the most profitable pharmaceutical company in the USA. He quotes Merck as saying 'We try never to forget that medicine is for the people. It is not for profits. The profits follow, and when we have remembered that, they have never failed to appear.'[21]

The principle of obliquity is the term used by John Kay to encapsulate this paradox of subsidiary focus defeating its objective if it comes into explicit or focal awareness. Kay borrows this term from James Black the chemist, whom Kay notes made more money for British companies than anyone else in the history of British business.[22] Black achieved this financial success by committing himself to work only for those companies that were more interested in chemistry than they were in profits. In essence, the principle of obliquity holds that some objectives are best pursued indirectly. Kay writes: 'When a characteristic is selected in an uncertain environment, deliberate action to promote the characteristic is often self-defeating.'[23] This observation has strong echoes of Polanyi's warning that we undermine our ability to achieve our objectives if we confuse subsidiary awareness with focal awareness.

To continue the analogy with the business world, to make the task of mission a focal awareness is akin to a business launching an advertising campaign which boasts that it intends to make huge profits. Such a campaign would have the opposite effect to the one intended. I suggest that effective mission is prone to the similar problem. Effective mission is not achieved by giving it focal awareness. Effective mission is a fruit – a gracious outcome of other factors working effectively and appropriately. This upends all our habits and assumptions. It means that effective mission is something that emerges as a result of looking and journeying outward rather than by means of a self-conscious and self-regarding process.

The art of leadership can be understood as the identification of a focal awareness around which we can organize our actions and which will operate obliquely to achieve our tacit and desired outcomes. This analysis is more than just a case of ensuring that we do not mistake the means for the end. It is about the recognition that some ends or objectives can never be achieved head on. For example a conscious effort to achieve happiness disintegrates into hedonism. In the context of lack of trust, attempting to recreate trust cannot be addressed head-on without falling prey to manipulation or even suspicion. The art, in complex circumstances, is to identify the oblique route by which one's objective can be achieved. This is the essence of the principle of obliquity.

Community ministry can provide an oblique route that can carry a focal awareness without undermining our tacit intention. Community ministry calls out a commitment to our neighbour and in expressing this commitment other tacit or subsidiary skills and resources flourish in an unself-conscious way. The emergent, virtuous processes that flow are more than just a product of our efforts because in partaking of God's economy of grace we become party to a cascade of grace that is far more generous and apposite than we could ever imagine. By journeying out in this way we will *find* ourselves creating church and being effective missioners. This virtuous process also enables us to acknowledge and understand that we receive our sight, or our truly Christian understanding, by embracing a struggle for righteousness and justice. It is via this journey outwards that we gain not only authenticity, but also begin to trust in the viability of God's economy which Jesus unfurls.

The real-life story from Hackney provides an illustration of the principle of obliquity in a very practical and unexpected way. The halls that were first used for the winter night shelter had roofs that leaked and kitchens and toilets that were an embarrassment. Two or three years later they have new or refurbished halls. Why? Because they had a story of local commitment that few funders and charitable trusts could resist; Sunday attendance has grown; they have other community ventures that have raised their profile and they are known in their local communities as a church, and as Christians 'who walk the talk'. These churches discovered that by being hospitable to the poor they glimpsed the reality and practicality of God's gracious economy.

Notes

1 The Methodist Church led the way with the report 'One Nation, One Gospel' in 1983; The Church of England published the report 'Faith in the City' in 1985 and the Episcopal Church in Scotland produced the report 'Blessed are the Poor' in 1988.

2 The report 'Faith in the City' was criticized by some for having a very thin theological section. The authors of the report were determined not to provide a complex theological treatise. Their case was twofold: the parable of the Good Samaritan gave an unsurpassed mandate to respond to those in need and theology must emerge out of our practice and our engagement rather than be generated by an uninvolved theologian sitting at a desk.

3 David Bosch, *Transforming Mission* (Maryknoll, New York: Orbis, 1991).

4 Martin Kähler, *Schriften zur Christologie und Mission* (Munich: Chr. Kaiser Verlag, 1974).

5 Bosch, op. cit., p. 378.

6 This theoretical or theological recognition has been less easy to translate into action. The question remains: How do we integrate work for justice with the recognition of Christ's unique saving power without drifting into the sequential process that has dominated for so long? This issue will be addressed in the course of this book.

7 The term 'social gospel' has often been used to undermine work of a social responsibility nature. The social gospel was most fully articulated in the USA at the turn of the twentieth century. Rauschenbusch and Ritschl were proponents of the idea of continuity between social progress and the Kingdom of God. The Kingdom of God would result from the evolutionary tendencies that were emerging in the progress being made by humankind through the application of professional expertise, techniques and organisation.

8 However, the intuitive resistance that these complaints point to may be more well founded than it is fashionable to admit. This reservation about social action and its place in the Church, especially when it is expressed as *meeting need*, deserves more thorough consideration. This will be addressed in the next chapter.

9 Mark 12.29–31. This summary of the Jewish Law that Jesus provides is more accommodating to those who exercise power than other examples of Jesus' teaching and actions. The focus on neighbour and self encourages person-to-person decency, which is commendable, but can obscure issues of justice and power. Clearly the emphasis on me and my neighbour provides an imperative to respond to the needs of my neighbour, however, as the Rich Young Ruler highlights, this summary of the Law provokes the question 'Who is my neighbour?' The term *neighbour* does not encourage the wider recognition of our fraternal relationships which are a product of having the same heavenly Father, and it is this that Jesus expressed and demonstrated in His daily life.

10 Conrad Boerma, *Rich Man, Poor Man and the Bible* (London: SCM, 1979).

11 Ibid., p. 10.

12 Ibid., p. 18.

13 Ibid., p. 19.

14 Ibid., p. 8.

15 Ways of helping us to rise above anxiety will be considered in chapter 9.

16 The issue of street homelessness in London is greatly contested. The Rough Sleepers Unit adjudged that the problem has been solved. Those closer to the ground consider this is an optimistic assessment.

17 I am grateful to Phillip Down for alerting me to the link between the principle of obliquity and the work of Michael Polanyi. See Michael Polanyi, *The Tacit Dimension* (London: Routledge and Kegan Paul, 1959).

18 Jerry H. Gill, *The Tacit Mode* (Albany: State University of New York, 2000), p. 34.

19 The same analysis could be applied to the process of being a church. Might 'church' be something that is best understood as a subsidiary awareness rather than a focal awareness? This would mean that we do church as a result of doing something else. For example, the need and longing to do and be church might result from a commitment to or experience of some kind of 'struggle'. Church therefore becomes a verb rather than a noun.

20 John Kay, 'Good Business', in his inaugural lecture for the Said Business School at Oxford, March 1998, p. 3.

21 Ibid., p. 3. I find it impossible to resist paraphrasing Merck: We (must) never forget that the Gospel is for the world. It is not for the Church. In pursuing the Gospel the process of being church will follow, and when we have remembered that, the Church has never failed.

22 James Black invented beta-blockers and anti-ulcerants.

23 Ibid., p. 4.

2

Community Ministry: More Than Meeting Need

Economists have already borrowed the concept of 'adaptive zones' from evolutionary biology. Joseph Schumpeter, in particular, drew parallels with the biologists' recognition of 'adaptive zones' in his economic models. He observed that times of economic boom occur when *swarms* of entrepreneurs try to implement an innovation at the same time. However, those who enter this new space and pursue the new opportunities discover that their business models, formed and nurtured by former practices and processes, are ill-adapted to cope with the new. Those who survive, and go on to flourish in the 'adaptive zone' are those who can also transform their structures and systems to accommodate the new opportunities.[1]

Schumpeter, and the evolutionary biologists from whom he borrowed the concept, might well have heeded Jesus' caution about new wine being stored in old wineskins. Christians can recite chapter and verse (in this instance Luke 6.37-9) about the need for renewing our processes or 'containers' if we are to receive and respond to the fresh, innovative good news that Jesus proclaimed. The temptation, therefore, might be to treat Schumpeter's insight as old hat. However, without discernment we can miss the possibility of having entered, or being on the brink of, an 'adaptive zone'; it is easy to miss the clues or fail to appreciate their significance. Schumpeter also warns that having identified an innovation there is a risk of 'swarming' as people rush to take advantage of the possibility of innovation and perceived advantage. At a time when we know we must find new ways of helping people to discover the Gospel, the danger of swarming, in pursuit of a perceived innovation, is something that we should heed.[2]

Schumpeter noted that after an economic boom associated with innovation the system has to correct itself, and this process weeds out those who have simply followed the leader without deeply appreciating the radicalness of the change that is required. Therefore, booms are often followed by bust. For example, Schumpeter's theory, despite dating back to the 1940s, has been applied to the dotcom boom, when newly formed companies gained rapidly in value in the anticipation of new profits being made in association with the internet. Such profits failed to materialize at the level predicted, and worse than this, practices were adopted to disguise the failure, contributing to a loss of trust and a loss of nerve as well as a loss of value.

It is not just economists that are wary of the danger of a boom being followed by bust. Biologists also note that the disruption, or loss of equilibrium, prompted by the innovatory leap into an adaptive zone can be so overwhelming to a species that the outcome might be negative. Adaptive zones, therefore, both for species and for organizations, involve both opportunities and risks. Avoiding the risks requires that the innovation associated with the adaptive zone must enhance the core functioning of the species or the purpose of the organization.

Over the last twenty years community involvement by churches has experienced a boom. Especially in poor communities projects and participation in neighbourhood forums have become an major part of the ministry of the local church. Previously, such involvement was often disdained and viewed as a potential distraction from the business of running a church. The demands for baptisms, weddings and funerals brought about sufficient contact with the community for most clergy and congregations. Now, there is a risk that churches have a sense of 'ought' in relation to community involvement, and this is the very dynamic that Schumpeter warns can prompt the swarming that pushes the system beyond boom and into bust.

To avoid the danger of bust, therefore, this innovatory aspect of church life must enhance the core functioning of the Church in the service of the Gospel. At a time when the Church is already fragile, it would be nothing short of disastrous to be tempted by siren calls that instil unproductive practices. It is essential, therefore, to examine the processes and practices associated with churches' involvement in their community in order to discern the good from the bad, creativity from thoughtless duplication and egotistical journeying from genuine struggle.

Examining our practices

Honest thinking and reflecting are essential to prevent a culture developing in the Church of *unexamined involvement* in community ministry. Failure to critique the growing community involvement by churches not only risks 'boom and bust'; it could obscure some exceedingly graceful dynamics that can flow from embracing a struggle for the well-being of our neighbour, and it can also risk betraying the primary task of the Church: that of helping people to discover the scope for relationship with God through Jesus.

I have a particular concern that unfettered and unthought commitment to community involvement or community ministry could contribute to an undermining of the local church itself. This concern has its roots in the years, long ago, when I studied sociology. In the 1970s, sociologists were greatly vexed by the persistence of church involvement in the USA. All other industrialized nations, especially those in Europe, evidenced a rapid decline in church attendance, and this fitted neatly with the idea of secularization being tied to the advancement of technology and economic success. It was, therefore, rather inconvenient to sociologists that the most economically successful nation should persist in bucking this trend. For in the USA the majority of people, regardless of income, class or colour, persisted in their church attendance. Even now, more than 30 years on, Americans continue to attend church and take their Christian faith very seriously.[3]

In order to rescue the secularization thesis sociologists had to account for this exception to their theorizing. There were two ways they tried to do this. The first was by emphasizing how religion is a source of security for the many, different, ethnic groups trying to get a foothold in a New World. The second rationale that sociologists used was that the churches in the USA have secularized themselves. They have become secularized from *within* by acting as voluntary organizations or adult education or leisure centres, rather than as a place for the development of faith and worship of God.

Those familiar with the practices of Willow Creek and other mega churches in the USA are to be forgiven for their disbelief that learned sociologists could persist with such an assumption and misrepresentation. However, it is to our benefit that we heed this warning. It may well be easier than we realize to secularize our churches from within. I write as someone who long before reading sociology had extracts of C. S. Lewis read to her at Sunday school. In particular I recollect the engaging Screwtape letters,[4] a great primer in relation to the wiles of Old Nick. I can imagine Uncle Screwtape, writing to his young nephew Wormwood, recommending that he distract the followers of Jesus by encouraging them into worthy activity that makes them feel good, and prevents them from recognizing and promoting the Gospel which Jesus expresses. There could be no better ruse to tempt the Church down a cul-de-sac.

In the intensely materialistic times in which we live, it is both easier, and in the world's terms more commendable, to develop provision for homeless people than it is to help people embrace faith and become church. The two are not mutually exclusive as Bosch points out, but all the pressures and temptations urge us into seeing and treating them as separate enterprises: so responding to need belongs to the voluntary sector with its commitment to good practice, networking and fund-raising from trusts and public agencies. Doing the God stuff belongs to the religious realm of prayer and piety and believing in miracles and the Bible. The ease with which we slip into these two cultures means that we rarely imagine being able to integrate them. For those involved in community ministry, the pressure to drift into becoming a voluntary provider of care and service is intense, and with this there comes the danger of secularizing the Church from within. To return to Schumpeter's analysis, this results in the ecclesiastical equivalent of economic bust.

Those stung by this analysis might respond with sound evidence that churches committed to community ministry as part of their mission strategy have grown (I in fact have done this in the previous chapter), and people who would not otherwise come to church have become open to the possibility of embracing faith in Jesus and a relationship with Him. I wholeheartedly agree that such evidence is emerging. However, I don't want us to be content with this, because the rush to provide such positive endorsement of community involvement betrays an inclination to put new wine in old wineskins. We have to sit lightly to the early indications that community ministry provides effective opportunities for mission, because this risks a return to a sequential model of mission that Bosch warned us against. The hazard is that the efficacy of community ministry as a method of pre-evangelism will reinforce a sequential model of mission which Bosch very clearly states is an inadequate expression of holistic mission. Furthermore, if we are bewitched by positive assessments of community ministry we risk the second maladaption: that of short-circuiting the exceedingly graceful dynamics that God has promised to us, but which are unavailable to us whilst ever we crave and possess power.

The distraction of a needs-meeting perspective

To head off these potential maladaptions it is important to interrogate our taken-for-granted first principles. In particular, to examine the basis of the practices adopted by churches in the 1970s and 80s when poor communities were disproportionately affected by hardship. The assumption that prevailed was that the local church should endeavour to meet the needs of local people. The principle and practice of *needs meeting* was taken for granted as a good thing. Armed with the example of the Good Samaritan, need meeting became the organizing principle for our community involvement. In support of this, community and parish audits were promoted as the sensible precursor to setting up a community project, and their focus was invariably to establish the needs of a community. Furthermore, the presentation of bids for financial support for community projects were, and still are, structured around the astute presentation of people's needs, and the capacity of the ensuing project to address these needs.

The liberal thinking that underpins a needs-meeting approach is based on the assumption that the application of rationality combined with reasonableness will result in progress, both in the social and scientific domains. This world view has its origins in the Enlightenment, when the capacity for Man to unravel and manipulate the natural phenomena became more and more reliable. The idea that social progress can be achieved by developing sensitive and informed social policies that address the needs of the poor has become the normative view. I grew up with this assumption, I have been shaped by this assumption and, like most others, I have adopted it in my practice.

However, this focus on needs meeting can cloud the significance of *participation* as a potentially transforming process. Community ministry projects are essentially participative structures. A structure of participation provides opportunities for people to take part in a wider struggle and the encounters that result can set up a transformational dynamic. A local church, in setting up a community ministry project, is inviting people to *participate in a struggle*. Community ministry, when stripped bare, is essentially a collection of rotas that enable people to contribute to a wider enterprise. The humble rota provides a structure for participation, and that participation provides people with experiences to reflect on, to mull over and, in due time, to be changed by. The potential transformational power of an invitation and opportunity to participate easily gets lost in the focus on needs meeting, which by definition requires one party in the encounter to be characterized as in some way deficient.

When a church or project gets caught up in a needs-meeting perspective it puts the Church and the congregation in a position of superiority. Those 'out there' are the ones in need, whilst those within the Church have the capacity to help. This may be a caricature, but nevertheless needs meeting as an aim must imply that those who are needy are in some way in deficit, whilst competence and resourcefulness are retained in the hands of the helper. The Gospel with its capacity to overturn everyday assumptions will have none of this. The gracious processes that Jesus demonstrates make it clear that it is the needy who carry the transformational potential. The radical actions of Jesus up-end the taken-for-granted pattern of giving and receiving. Furthermore, unless we can free ourselves from the liberal mantra of needs meeting, we may miss the real blessings and gracefulness associated with journeying out – without the expectation of being able to meet people's needs.

Let me stress very clearly that there is no problem with establishing a project as a response to a perceived need in the community, for example, providing hospitality for recently arrived asylum seekers in a neighbourhood, or in response to a high proportion of frail, elderly people in the parish. Such expression of care is to be commended and cherished. The problem of 'needs meeting' begins to arise when the provision being made goes beyond hospitality, and the complexity of the needs of the 'clients' starts to be recognized. At this point, the project may *automatically* assume it has to respond by providing a greater diversity of services and a more professional approach to its work. The temptation is to drift into a feeling of obligation to pursue the needs of the client group, and the decision to develop additional provision in order to respond more adequately to the needs of clients is hard to challenge. Only the most hardhearted could speak against such a commitment, and that may be precisely the trap for churches. The urge to meet the client's needs more thoroughly is beyond rebuke, but it may indicate a failure of the imagination and confidence in the transforming power of God.

The radical, missionary activity of the Church cannot, like liberal, secular, social policy, aim at the transformation of the poor. In the new adaptive zone we have entered, the aim must be the transformation of the secure, the well-meaning and the well-endowed of this world. The processes that Jesus teaches and demonstrates invest potential in the most un-likely, not in the well resourced. Focusing on 'needs meeting' is at odds with the coaching and urging that we receive from Jesus to take seriously the reality of Gospel reversals. The ways of Jesus are not the ways of the world, but they are not a fairy story either. Gospel reversals are to be taken seriously. The challenge is to have the imagination, trust, expectation and capacity to facilitate situations where the upside-down nature of God's kingdom can prosper.

Preoccupation with needs can mask a host of graceful, kingdom dynamics that can be set in train when those who are secure, and apparently competent, encounter those who know the demands and limitations of a life marked by struggle. To illustrate the things that can get missed by emphasizing needs meeting, I return to the example of the churches' winter night shelters referred to in the previous chapter. If people's minds and practice are dominated by a needs-meeting philosophy, then the outcomes of the ventures will be assessed in terms of:

♦ the number of meals served;
♦ the number of 'bed-nights' offered;
♦ the number of rough sleepers using the facilities regularly;
♦ the number of asylum seekers;
♦ the number using the facilities in terms of gender and age;
♦ volunteers' perceptions of needs in addition to those of homelessness, for example mental illness, drug or alcohol addiction;
♦ clients' stated preference for type of accommodation;
♦ the needs the project fulfils in relation to the volunteers.

Without question such an evaluation of how a project meets clients' needs is valuable, and clearly can provide an important foundation for providing a more sensitive and better-equipped project. So, for example, the pursuit of a needs-meeting approach would mean that those responsible for the winter night shelter would soon be taking steps to make better provision for homeless people. Instead of continuing to make provision in battered church halls the challenge becomes setting up more hostels with trained staff and access to a range of rehabilitation programmes. However, with this comes the likelihood of a reduction in the number of volunteers and an emphasis on employing more staff. This brings about a subtle change in the pattern of responsibility and relationships, and a net loss in terms of people participating in a struggle for the well-being of others. Furthermore, the distinction between helped and helper gets reinforced and the relationships between the two groups change. The perception that people care because they are paid to do so enters the equation and the potential for graceful relationships is inhibited.

To use a colloquial expression, a local church can 'lose the plot' when faced with the pressure to develop a more responsive, quasi-professional provision. The perceived next stage in the development of the project opens it to the *mores*[5] of the voluntary sector, as the threshold between *community ministry project* and *voluntary organization* is crossed. Some would argue that the gain from the further development of the project accrues to the homeless people. Common sense suggests this will be the case, but the balance of gains and losses may be less clear than is thought.

Weber's 'iron cage of bureaucracy'

As care for the needy becomes formalized it gathers more bureaucratic or, to use Max Weber's term, it faces 'legal rational' constraints. Max Weber, although writing more than 100 years ago, coined the term 'iron cage of rationality' to describe this dynamic. With a sense of foreboding Weber anticipated the implications of defensive bureaucracy on the formal provision of care. The application of rationality to caring could be described as a virus that enters our corporate efforts. The source of this virus is the clash of *legitimate* interests in the enterprise. Those in need have legitimate interests but so too do those who are employed to care. Likewise the agency providing the care has a legitimate interest in distributing its provision as well as possible in the context of scarce resources. Over time, this contest between justifiable and legitimate interests is most likely to be resolved in favour of the best resourced and powerful. Whilst employees have some sanction against the overriding demands of their employers, in that in the last resort they can withdraw their labour, the clients of the agency have no such sanction. Over time, the vested interests or desires of those on the inside of the organization triumph.[6]

Those of us who have earned our living in the 'caring professions' may occasionally reflect on the balance of benefit between the professional carer and the needy client. Despite our best efforts to make it otherwise, the benefits associated with professional provision repeatedly benefit the professional cadre more than they do the needy. Weber's 'iron cage of rationality' provides an insight into the phenomenon of structural sin, for it exposes how our well-meaning efforts invariably involve a contest of interests, and even when this contest is resolved in a reasonable and rational manner, repeatedly the losers in this contest are those who are poor.

Weber's use of the term *iron cage* emphasizes the constraining force that bears down on those who would wish to express care in a spontaneous rather than formalized way. The worldly-wise practices of risk assessments, health and safety regulations, data protection and child protection, to name but a few, are unarguably useful developments. In fact they are impossible to argue against and inescapable, and this makes the virus all the more virulent. So many, top professionals in the caring agencies now grieve that their role is no longer to enhance the delivery of care but rather to maintain the *defensive bureaucracy* that surrounds their agency. In a world where rational systems and legal rights predominate there is a stark equation: the more complex and professional the provision being made, the more defensive the organization's bureaucracy will become, in response to the fear of litigation should its representatives fail to meet its explicit, high standards.

Not only does formalized provision quickly become caught up in the rules and regulations that characterize defensive bureaucracy, there is also the issue of *opportunity* cost. Opportunity cost is an economic concept. It highlights how in a world of scarce resources there is a cost in choosing one option rather than another. The cost is in relation to the choice that has to be forgone.[7] When a modest, but participative community ministry project embarks upon a process of formalizing its provision and becoming more professional, the opportunity cost is rarely acknowledged. In particular, those of us who are interested in the mission of the Church and the Kingdom of God have been slow to recognize the costs associated with this change in emphasis. By allowing ourselves to be dominated by the assumption that to respond effectively to need requires more and more professionalism, we overlook the graceful possibilities associated with informality and being alongside *without power*. In fact, the failure to recognize and value the gains associated with *amateur* provision has been little short of a calamity.

Grace cascades

We have been slow to recognize that when people, motivated by venturesome love, embrace a struggle for the well-being of others, it can prompt a very graceful, and often unanticipated dynamic, a *cascade of grace*, and this dynamic should be the very thing that churches are seeking to generate. The churches involved in the winter night shelters provide hospitality for homeless people for just one night a week for twelve weeks a year, and the very modesty of this enables some escape from the 'iron cage of rationality'. Reliance on voluntary commitment means that what is offered is a welcome and food and shelter but it provokes countless internal conversations within each person, whether volunteer or one who seeks shelter. This ability to provoke reflection is an important aspect of the cascade of grace that is set in train. For example,

♦ Those who help with practical tasks (often the friends and neighbours of the key volunteers) are invited to the carol service and the Christmas party for everyone involved including the homeless people. Here the cascade of grace gains momentum: residents of the neighbourhood start to know homeless people – to know their name and to know some of their story – and in knowing something of their story, the inclination to blame the homeless for their plight begins to fall away.

♦ The Christmas story is contextualized – and refreshed. In the context of the winter night shelter, everyone, the homeless and the householder alike, knows the implications of there being no room at the inn. When a Gospel story and a personal story coincide, it often creates a powerful dynamic, sometimes even triggering a religious experience.

♦ Those who wash and iron the sheets each week begin to pray for those who will be lying in them; respectable householders begin to cherish homeless people and prayer gets into the equation and thus triggers a further cascade of grace.

♦ The experience of discipleship provokes a deeper awareness of personal sin and recognition of our (the respectable!) complicity in sinful systems. Discipleship ceases to be understood as 'good works and meeting needs'. Rather discipleship fosters a growth of humility and recognition of our inadequacy,[8] both personal and corporate, and on occasion, it is about having one's heart broken.

♦ The local Members of Parliament get invited to a meeting of all the helpers and the homeless people to discuss the high level of homelessness in the neighbourhood. One can only speculate about the impact this has on them, possibly the shock of their lives. More than 100 people turned up: church members, those who washed and ironed sheets, baked, washed up, as well as those who were homeless. The authenticity of people's experience was palpable. Homeless people had a voice and commanded key places on the platform and at the microphone. The plight of asylum seekers was spoken of with compassion, and consternation expressed that the best that seemed to be available for them were battered church halls – and it wasn't good enough, not for anyone, and certainly not for those who were traumatized and with little children.

♦ The MPs were virtually lost for words and pledged themselves to be more active on the issue of homelessness in the future. One can only speculate, but the following day they might have been anything but subdued. One can imagine in the Members' bar they might have regaled fellow MPs with the story of the previous night with a church packed with constituents and homeless people. They might have speculated, jokingly of course, that another religious revival was on the cards. Maybe privately, they would have noted never again to go to a meeting called by the churches without doing some homework first.

With just these few illustrations it becomes possible to see the virtuous or Godly processes that can be set in train if we are prepared to see beyond a needs-meeting perspective. We start to understand community ministry as a place where:

♦   the poor transform the rich;
♦   simple responses enable some freedom from the limitations of caring in a legal-rational or bureaucratic context;
♦   a new theory of action can be explored based on Gospel insights;
♦   opportunities are created to express discipleship;
♦   anxiety and resentment can be addressed in healthy ways.

These are some of the distinctive outcomes of community ministry if the *practicality* of the Kingdom reversals that Jesus both proclaimed and demonstrated are taken seriously and acted upon.

A Christian theory of action

To counteract the dominance of a needs-meeting approach it is important to articulate a theory of action based on a Gospel model of change and development. Alasdair MacIntyre's insights are helpful in relation to this task. The central motif of MacIntyre's famous book, *After Virtue*[9] is that it is essential that we find a way to articulate what is our human *telos*,[10] and endeavour to make our actions consistent with it. However, in a post-modern world, MacIntrye observes that both our cultural life and any sense of moral coherence has fragmented.[11] This means moral language, and the moral concepts to which it refers, exist only as fragments of a once coherent account. Over time, these moral fragments have come to seem arbitrary, and are treated as expressions of power of one group over another, or simply the product of emotions that are unrelated to anything of substance.

Faith communities are the exception to this because of persisting with the idea that the human enterprise has a purpose. Before the Enlightenment, the dominance of religious belief meant that people could have provided, with some conviction:

♦ an assessment of humanity as we are;
♦ a description of humanity as we should be;
♦ how we can get from where we are to where we should be.[12]

MacIntrye questions the future viability of the human enterprise if we refuse to acknowledge moral imperatives that enable humankind to get from the reality of how we are to the potential that we could or should be. MacIntrye is not saying that in pre-Enlightenment times people had the right answers to the 'is/ought' dilemma that is the basis of moral action. He urges us to take seriously the historical journey that ideologies and philosophies have taken, and in particular he exposes the twists and turns that the Church has taken. In particular MacIntyre notes the extent to which, in our history, we have promoted an obligation to the Church rather than a response to the Gospel.

The fragile remnant that we experience as church now has been purged of its power and status. The processes unleashed by the Enlightenment have brought about this harsh pruning. This increased distance from power and influence, the liberation theologian, Gutiérrez suggests, has brought about a new capacity to understand a Gospel-shaped *telos*, or purpose for humankind.[13] This opportunity for a new perspective on the unchanged message of Jesus is a further aspect of the adaptive zone that the Church has entered. Now the radical processes that Jesus commends and demonstrates are no longer obscured by the Church's dependence on worldly power. Now the response to the foundational question around which a theory of action is built can be judged against a controversial Gospel. The theory of action that each of us chooses to adopt will be based on our assessment of what is it we have *to do* in moving from our current state to one that is closer to our purpose, or *telos*.

My understanding of the *telos*, or purpose of the human

enterprise is that we are called by God to struggle for a tender relationship with Him and our fellows, aware of our brokenness and aware of His graciousness towards us. In our post-modern world, each one of us has the (lonely) scope to articulate the human *telos* for ourselves. In previous eras, to have done this, in contradiction to Mother Church, would have warranted being burnt at the stake. I offer my version of the human *telos* with the expectation that it will be modified and reshaped, not just by others, but also by myself, as new insights and reflections have an impact. A theory of action is a transient construction. It is something that gets superseded as new ideas win the day. It is a working tool that links general, day-to-day actions with our understanding of the end or purpose of the human enterprise and it enables one option to be prioritized over another.[14] Without a theory of action, it is difficult to avoid drifting into populism, traditionalism or simply drifting. One's theory of action is not a sacrosanct creed. It should be applied, reflected upon, modified and even ultimately replaced

In scientific disciplines and within the social sciences, it is acknowledged that understanding and practice advances through a process of building, testing and elaborating theories. This is not so in relation to theology or mission, where we almost manifest contempt for such an approach. However, a theory must not be confused with dogma. In the case of dogma, our habit is to live by it, defend it and justify it. In the case of a theory of action we should cherish it but also question it, for a theory of action is expendable. A theory of action enables some actions to be given priority above others but when new information or opportunities emerge it must remain open to amendment.

The theory of action that I offer as an alternative to a needs-meeting approach has three elements. These elements relate to our specific context and are robust enough to be a basis for specific actions, and these actions I suggest move us in the direction of the radical transformation that Jesus promises. The first element is:

The importance of struggle to the kingdom of God and the well-being of the children of God.

We have been seduced into believing that we can organize our lives around the pursuit of pleasure and leisure. We are the first generation in human history where this fantasy dominates to the extent that we assume such easy living is the norm. Thus we fail to recognize that for 99 per cent of human history, and for two-thirds of the world's population, *struggle* is an essential motif. To eschew plenty and pleasure and actively pursue grief and hardship is clearly perverse. We cannot undo our context as citizens of wealthy, Western nations. However, those of us who do live comfortable lives, can, through our capacity for empathy, engage in struggle *by proxy*. This is what discipleship is all about.

The very notion of discipleship implies struggle; the notion that the world is in travail as it reaches for the fulfilment that God has promised also implies struggle. Furthermore, biologists tell us that for every species survival through the earthly evolutionary journey requires struggle. The avoidance of struggle has profound repercussions for our spirituality and theological understanding, for the hope of the Kingdom of God on this earth and for the very survival of the species *Homo sapiens*.

Given this centrality of struggle, our churches have a pastoral responsibility to provide structures that enable people to engage in struggle, or to use another code, to express the *venturesome love* that Karl Rahner suggests is at the heart of discipleship.[15] Some minimal structure that enables active participation is essential if discipleship of the venturesome-love kind is to be tangible and move beyond pious words and naive optimism. The churches' winter night shelters are an excellent example of structures that facilitate people's engagement in struggle on behalf of others.

The second element of the theory of action is:

To take seriously the mysterious part which those who are poor and marginalized have in the purposes of God.

This element is rooted in the undeniable emphasis in the Gospels on the significance of the poor. The repeated reference to those who are poor and excluded is a unique feature of Christ's actions and teaching. It therefore behoves His followers at least to give credence to the mysterious and purposeful role of those who know deeply the reality of struggle.

One speculates, supported by insights from liberation theology, that this mysterious purpose may be to do with the potential for transformation that comes from drawing alongside those who are poor and marginalized. This extraordinarily graceful dynamic may be an important missionary force in enabling Christians and non-Christians to take seriously the alternative *economy* that is at the heart of the Gospel. How else are we to understand and have confidence in the reversals that Jesus urged us to take seriously? How else are we to collaborate with God in bringing about His Kingdom on earth?

Being alongside the poor and marginalized is akin to George MacLeod's recognition that in this world there are thin places (for George Macleod, the founder of the Iona Community, Iona was for him one of these places), where only a tissue separates us from a deep sense of God's presence. Our missionary endeavours, therefore, have to harness the enigmatic ability of the most unlikely and vulnerable to generate a force that moves us closer to the kingdom of God – and to God Himself. To develop holistic mission we have to foster encounters which carry the likelihood of transformation of the apparently secure, comfortable and competent, who in the world's terms have successful lives.

However, there is a danger in emphasising the transformational capacity of the poor, for it can easily degenerate into a romanticism that is both unrealistic and entrapping. To lessen this danger our churches and community ministry projects need to be places where reflection on experience is encouraged. Therefore, we must not just be alongside the poor, we must also *reflect* on the experience of being alongside the poor, and through this acknowledge the sinful limitations that dog us all, rich and poor alike. It is this reality and pervasiveness of sin that leads to the third element of the theory of mission that I commend:

To take seriously the implications of the fact that we are all brothers and sisters with the same Heavenly Father.

The significance of this glorious element at the heart of our faith must be taken seriously. It is not just vain rhetoric; it is a practical and also deeply challenging feature of our faith. The fraternal relations that Jesus makes possible, for He is our brother, requires us to continually work to ensure that our relationships reflect this gracious gift. James Alison suggests that one of the first obligations that we carry in relation to our brothers and sisters is to rise above resentment.[16] This is a realistic, although demanding task. Resentment, unlike many other emotions, is one which we can recognize within ourselves, and identify the person or persons against whom it is directed. The specificity and tangible nature of resentment in comparison with emotions such as rejection, anxiety and anger means that resentment is palpable and knowable. This gives us a handle on the emotion. Being able to recognize when resentment is building up within us provides us with the option of yielding and giving in to the negativity or working to rise above it and free ourselves from it. In giving way to resentment we are guilty of fratricide, the destruction of the fraternal relations that God, in enabling us to call him 'Our Father', has given to us.

Alison offers us countless insights into Jesus' commitment to avoid resentment even when confronted by those who had opted to be His enemies.[17] Resentment of our God-given brothers and sisters is a capital sin, that is, a sin from which so many other sins flow. Resentment spawns hatred and deceit, and resentment is the very opposite to grace.[18] Following Bosch's urging that we take seriously the *life* of Jesus as well as His death and resurrection, in attending to the life of our brother Jesus, we see that He endeavoured to do all that He could to maintain fraternal relations.

If part of God's gift to us, in addition to salvation through his Son, is that we can also call God Father, the implication of this is quite delightful and quite profound. Whereas our culture might teach us to see people as strangers, and emotionally we will experience the threat of and anxiety provoked by strangers, the graciousness of God, who wants us all as His children, is such that we are invited to journey out and discover and encounter not strangers but brothers and sisters. The horizontal relationships, i.e. relationships with our God-given brothers and sisters, are thus a reflection of the vertical relationship with God our Father. The lifetime example of Jesus and His extending fraternal relationship to everyone, especially to the Gentiles and those considered unclean, and his refusal to give way to resentment is a theme which runs through Jesus' life as strongly as his commitment to the poor.

This theory of action that I propose aims to take account of the specific pressures and predilections of our Western, postmodern context. We have to rise above the temptations of decadent self-indulgence and opt to embrace the struggle against all that coerces and damages God's creation and God's children. We have to take seriously the possibility that being alongside those who are poor and who know deeply the reality of struggle may be a thin place where God reveals himself in a very mysterious and indisputable way. The underpinning for this is the gift that God our Father gives us, that in allowing and enabling us to be His children we are not strangers but brothers and sisters. To partake of this gracious gift we have to do battle with the resentment that so easily bubbles up when our fragile egos get threatened by others.

I also suggest that this theory enables us to get beyond the narrowness of the needs-meeting philosophy that dominates so much of our thinking. Our engagement with those who are locked in struggle is based on the expression of fraternal relations, it is the route to a thin place where God promises He will meet us, and it is a school of relating where we can practise freeing ourselves from resentment and other demeaning aspects of fallen humanity. But there is more. I also suggest that it enables us to partake of the graciousness of God's economy or providence that is associated with His Kingdom. I have alluded to what I have come to describe as God's gracious economy on a number of occasions so far. When we engage in struggle on behalf of others, especially when both we and the other are empty-handed,[19] then we become party to a cascade of grace. Deep, generous and surprising blessings come when we follow the instructions that are clearly given by Jesus. However, just like the servants at the wedding at Cana, we too have to take Jesus seriously when He suggests things that seem to be at odds with common sense and the ways of the world.

Notes

1 Joseph A. Schumpeter, *Essays on Entrepreneurs, Innovations, Business Cycles and the Evolution of Capitalism*, (ed.) Richard V. Clemence (New Brunswick, NJ: Transaction Publishers, 1992). Schumpeter's most influential works were *The Theory of Economic Development* (Cambridge, Mass.: Harvard University Press, 1934) and *Capitalism, Socialism and Democracy* (New York: Harper, 1950). For a more recent application of Schumpeter's theory see Richard R. Nelson and Sidney G. Winter, *An Evolutionary Theory of Economic Change* (Cambridge, Mass.: Harvard University Press, 1982).

2 The most extensive evidence on this point comes from the history of intelligence failures in relation to international relations. A consistent theme in retrospective

studies is that failure occurs not because the intelligence system failed to acquire warning signals but because it failed to process, relate and interpret those signals into a message that could inform actions. Cf Roberta Wohlstetter's study of the Pearl Habour Attack, *Pearl Habor, Warning and Decision* (Stanford: Stanford University Press, 1962) and more recently, the failure of the Security Services in the USA to take appropriate action in response to warnings of al-Qa'eda inspired terrorism prior to the assault on the 'Twin Towers'.

3 The fact that such a high proportion of Americans are keen and active Christians causes me much heart searching. It forces me to ponder whether extensive allegiance to Christ is worth anything at all in relation to the struggle for the Kingdom of God. With so many Christians is there anything distinctly commendable about the USA – other than a 'go-getting' mentality? This highlights for me the vagueness of our talk about working for the Kingdom of God and the inadequacy of our vision for human flourishing. Now that would be a bold theme for a book!

4 C. S. Lewis, *The Screwtape Letters* (London: Geoffrey Bles, 1942).

5 I use the term *mores* in order to emphasize that there are distinct behaviours and approaches associated with the voluntary sector. Many aspects of the good practice within the voluntary sector would be a welcome addition to church life – for example, clear accountability structures, active pursuit of equal opportunities and active commitment to empowerment of 'clients', to mention just some.

6 We need to note well that this virus affects all institutions, not just voluntary and statutory organizations. In fact, one could make a case that this virus is present in its most well-adapted form within the established Church.

7 The concept of opportunity cost in economics deserves a theological counterpart: original sin perhaps?

8 For example, when the volunteer on the door of the

church hall has to turn people away because all the camp beds are allocated.

9 Alasdair MacIntyre, *After Virtue: A Study in Moral Theory* (Notre Dame: University of Notre Dame Press, 1984).

10 *Telos* is a Greek word meaning the goal, the end or purpose of the human enterprise.

11 MacIntyre stresses the distinction between pluralism and fragmentation. Pluralism describes a world with competing outlooks, traditions or claims to the truth. It implies that each culture can be articulated in a coherent and differentiated manner, and the differences between these rival 'plausibility structures' can be identified and debated. Fragmentation, on the other hand, is, according to MacIntrye, a far more challenging phenomenon, marked by incoherence and lives that are shaped by piecemeal, idiosyncratic values, leading to a sense of the world as 'fallen apart'.

12 Ibid., p. 54.

13 Gustavo Gutiérrez, *A Theology of Liberation* (Fifteenth anniversary edition with new Introduction by the author) (Maryknoll, New York: Orbis, 1988, p. xlv).

14 A theory of action is an essential tool for clergy. Clergy have more 'disposable' time than any other occupational group. Without a theory of action it is impossible to make use of this disposable time purposefully. Ouch!

15 K. Rahner, *Theological Investigations XI* (London: Darton, Longman and Todd, 1974).

16 James Alison, *Faith Beyond Resentment* (London: Darton, Longman and Todd, 2001).

17 In particular, Alison's reflection on John 8.31-59, when Jesus is teaching in the treasury in the Temple, is particularly illustrative. See *Faith Beyond Resentment*, pp. 58-74.

18 Ibid., p. 44.

19 Jayakumar Christian, in his book *God of the Empty-Handed* (Monrovia, California: MARC, 1999), emphasizes the transforming potency of a deep encounter with the powerless poor.

3

Social Capital – the *Big* Idea

Every so often, a new idea enters the arena of social and economic policy that generates new approaches and insights. Social capital is an example of this. Interest in the concept of social capital cuts across the political ideologies of both Left and Right. For example both New Labour and the Right-wing Bush administration in the USA have embraced the concept and used it to inform their policies. In fact, confidence in this new idea is such that social policies that have been in place for over 50 years are being overturned in order to encourage the growth of social capital. Social capital also happens to be extremely significant to the Church – and the Gospel, because social capital is essentially about trust and the ability and willingness to cross boundaries between strangers.

> Take for example the mum with a babe in buggy and an 'under-five' by her side as she is confronted by the 29 steps that must be negotiated to get on to the tube at Brixton Underground station. A fellow traveller sees her plight and takes hold of the front of the buggy and together they negotiate the steps. Mum anxiously bidding child number two to follow closely behind. However, child number two is reluctant to face all those steps single-handed and plunge into the great sea of people coming up the stairs towards her. She freezes and starts to cry. Another stranger coming up the stairs quickly reads the situation and comes alongside the sobbing

child. He offers her, not his hand (very large), but his finger
for her to hold on to so that together they can catch up with
Mum.

A scene similar to this is probably repeated every ten minutes
in Brixton. It involves complete strangers making a split
second decision to respond to others in need. In Brixton it is
particularly striking because people of different nationalities,
faiths and colours take account of the immediate need of
those who are very different from them. This type of attentiveness to the needs of others has gone on throughout
history and throughout the world, but never before in the
English-speaking world has it been honoured with a technical
label and subjected to such close analysis. The bad news is
that the reason for this analysis is that such day-to-day attentiveness to the needs of others is in sharp decline.

When social bonds fray, the loss of mutual concern and
attentiveness to the needs of others carries a real, and meas-
urable, cost. Social capital not only enhances our communal
lives, it also has an economic value. Francis Fukuyama in his
book *The Great Disruption* observes that whilst a culture of
intensive individualism may contribute to innovation and
market growth, when it spills over into the realm of social
norms, it corrodes virtually all forms of authority and weakens
the bonds that hold families, neighbourhoods and even
nations together.[1] Whilst in the past, those who bewailed a
loss of neighbourliness and sense of community belonging
might have been considered hopelessly nostalgic and out of
touch now it is recognized that such intangible attributes
such as our social ties make people more productive. This
makes social capital one of those rare phenomena which is
both a 'private good' and a 'public good' – with economic
consequences.

The example of the young mum receiving assistance in
Brixton illustrates this. She and the stranger who considers
her needs are involved in a private transaction. But if such
encounters evaporated it would have public consequences:

the costly redesign of Underground stations; the requirement to have more station staff to assist passengers. These things may in fact be very desirable but they come at a cost. For the users of the Underground the extent to which they assist each other rather than walk by on the other side, ultimately gets translated into a higher or lower cost of a ticket. And if the managers of the Underground decide that mums with young children are not a priority then there are other repercussions at both a private and public level. Mums as individuals, i.e. at a private level, face more isolation and stress with the public consequence of greater cost to the National Health Service. It is perhaps not surprising, therefore, that in Britain it is reported to be the Chancellor of the Exchequer who is keenest to promote policies that increase the level of social capital.

The nuts and bolts of social capital

All of us are involved in making a judgement about whom we can trust whether it be in relation to neighbours, businesses or traders. This is the basis of *reputation*, and a person's reputation shapes the actions of others. If people are inclined to ascribe negative or dodgy reputations to others this prompts a haemorrhage of trust and disrupts relationships in all kinds of ways.[2] This means that a society with a high level of trust is more efficient than a distrustful society because trustworthiness underpins the reciprocal relationships between people and this 'lubricates' social life.

Reciprocal relationships can take two forms:

'I'll do this for you - if you do that for me.'

This is referred to as *specific* reciprocity.

An illustration of specific reciprocity is provided by the British Heart Foundation campaign to encourage the public to know what to do if someone has a heart attack. Their campaign featured two posters adjacent to each other, the first posing the question 'Would you know what to do if the person next to you had a heart attack?' And the second poster posing the question 'Would the person next to you know what to do if you had a heart attack?' Specific reciprocity is essentially motivated by self-interest and it is the basis of trade, whether it be by barter or by credit card.

The second form of reciprocal relationship is:

'I'll do this for you ...' without expecting anything in return.

This is referred to as *generalized* reciprocity.

In the example from Brixton Underground station the person helping to carry the buggy and the guy who provided the escort for the fearful youngster acted without self-interest. In fact they put themselves to inconvenience. (This is no exaggeration in the context of dense crowds and steep and numerous steps.) Their actions are an example of *generalized reciprocity* for there is no anticipation of receiving anything back in return.[3] It is this generalized reciprocity that is so valuable to our social life and our sense of being at home in the world, or at least the neighbourhood.

Social capital is built up from the generalized and specific acts of reciprocity between people. However, these acts of reciprocity can be limited to those who are one's friends, one's extended family or one's ethnic group or social class. In order to get a full overview of the concept of social capital it is therefore also necessary to take account of how our allegiances have an impact.

Bonding social capital involves strong allegiances between people, and through this commitment to each other support and solidarity can be carried. Church membership could sometimes be described in this way. Noticeably, different denominations and groupings have varying degrees of bonding or solidarity. Putnam suggests[4] that bonding social capital acts like *social glue*, in that it has the capacity to hold or bind people together. This leads him to talk not just of bonding social capital but of *exclusive* social capital. From a sociological point of view, being part of such a bonded group is good for 'getting by' in that the solidarity which is created within the group can provide support for those in the group who are having a hard time. However, it also has the effect of reinforcing a narrow understanding and sense of who we are, and when solidarity is narrowly focused it can provoke resentment of the stranger. Bonding social capital, although it reassures people when the going gets tough and it can contribute to a sense of community, does not encourage people to journey out, confident that the stranger can also be their brother or sister. Whilst bonding social capital creates strong in-group loyalty, such solidarity can have the effect of creating antagonism with those who perceive themselves as outside the group, and the feeling of being outside a strongly bonded group or community can provoke resentment.

Putnam warns 'Sometimes "social capital", like its conceptual cousin "community", sounds warm and cuddly ... we need to beware of a treacly sweet "Kumbaya" interpretation. Networks and the associated norms of reciprocity are generally good for those inside the network, but the external effects of social capital are by no means always positive.'[5] Putnam cites the example of Timothy McVeigh who blew up the Federal Building in Oklahoma City, helped by his network of friends who were bound together by shared values and a sense of reciprocity in each other. If Putnam were to write today his analysis would no doubt include the al-Qa'eda movement and its actions on 11 September 2001.

Although bonding social capital has a clear downside it does have powerful, positive, social effects. It provides a network that can deliver support in both routine and the most arduous of contexts: 'Need a car to visit your brother in hospital in Somerset? Here take mine'; 'Let me babysit for you. You and your husband deserve a night out'; 'I'll sort out that virus on your computer'. These examples sound distinctly suburban, but bonding social capital is present amongst those who are homeless, drug addicts and prisoners. I share a humbling example – again from those 29 steps that have to be negotiated at Brixton Underground station.

Vikki is well known in Brixton. She sits on two crates and displays her paintings – usually of fish or fruit. Her paintings are garish with plenty of coloured, glitter paint and surrounded by hologram Sellotape. She sells a good number because of their primitive charm. She also plays amazingly tunefully and loudly on a comb and paper, beating out an accompanying rhythm with her foot and by shaking the coins in the plastic throwaway cup with which she is collecting. She is possibly the most successful of the busker-beggars at Brixton.

One evening I found myself following Vikki up the 29 steps at the Underground station. I noticed that spontaneously she had reached out to a very woebegone man struggling up the steps ahead of her. Possibly he had had a stroke to add to the distress of his homelessness. Into his hand Vikki put a pound coin.

Social capital, therefore, like other powerful phenomena, has the capacity for both good and ill. Those of us with a religious commitment need to heed this warning, for we must not assume that the social capital that is generated by religious commitment is always virtuous, and in particular, a commitment to fraternal relations requires us to move beyond bonding social capital and embrace *bridging* social capital.

Bridging social capital extends trust to beyond one's own network, and encourages smooth relations with strangers. For this reason Putnam refers to bridging social capital as *inclusive* social capital. Bridging social capital leads to a broadening of people's identities because it requires journeying out to engage with the stranger. Bridging social capital is less prevalent than bonding social capital, and it is diminishing.

Social capital and local communities

The level of social capital is different for different countries and variations exist at very local levels. For example, William Julius Wilson in his book *The Truly Disadvantaged*[6] focuses on the significance of reciprocal behaviour in poor communities. In his analysis he identifies the pressures that contribute to the formation of a geographically based underclass, and he concludes that it is the loss of social capital that is the critical contributor to the negative sub-culture which characterizes an underclass. He begins his analysis by focusing on the regular demographic changes that occur in any neighbourhood. At certain stages there will be a larger number of young people than at others, and when this happens there is a greater likelihood of the emergence of a group of youngsters (traditionally young boys) who indulge in antisocial behaviour. This leads to established residents feeling under threat, less secure, more anxious and, therefore, motivated to move. Those who reoccupy the area are unable to exercise reciprocal behaviour in the same way as longstanding neighbours. The impact of this is that people feel even more uneasy, the neighbourhood gets the reputation of going downhill, and that reputation adds energy to the downward spiral.

In the language of social capital what happens in this situation is that the *radius of social trust* has shortened, and continues to do so as the negative reputation gains momentum. The newcomers get scapegoated as adding to the problem and this inclines the remaining longstanding residents to be less neighbourly with newcomers and so the level of reciprocity in the neighbourhood plummets. Perception and reality feed off each other and a downward spiral culminates in a hard-to-let estate or shunned inner city.

The significance of neighbourliness and trust within a local community has now been recognized in government policymaking. The most extensive expression in the UK of a policy shaped by the need to enhance social capital is 'Neighbourhood Renewal'. The poorest 10 per cent of wards in England are the focus of these community-led, regeneration programmes. Whilst in previous decades the fear was that dependence on welfare would corrupt people's willingness to seek employment, now the fear is that dependence on welfare undermines reciprocal behaviour, and its close cousin, civil society. The policy of Neighbourhood Renewal encourages local people to plan and sometimes run some of the public services in their locality. These opportunities to participate in shaping public services and work for the benefit of others are all aimed at increasing or lengthening the radius of social trust in communities where reciprocity has evaporated.

This commitment to community-led regeneration involves powers and responsibilities being delegated to smaller-scale groupings so that citizens and local communities manage more and more aspects of their neighbourhood life, leaving governments (both nationally and locally) to concentrate on strategic planning and coordination. Everything possible is now being done to encourage people to participate in local issues to counteract the inclination of people to see themselves as consumers or recipients of services. The fear is that, unless active steps are taken, in the not too distant future the generosity of spirit that prompts generalized reciprocity will dry up. However, there are question marks over what kind of incentives will motivate other-regarding and sometimes self-denying behaviour that is so essential to the growth of social capital.

Social analysts in Britain do not believe that the churches will ever regain sufficient momentum to be able to capture the hearts and minds of anything but an insignificant minority. Added to this, the perception that predominates is that the faith communities generate bonding rather than bridging social capital, and in a mobile, diverse society this is a liability rather than a strength. For this reason, the government's favoured mechanism through which to regenerate social capital is by promoting voluntary organizations and community groups. This strategy risks overestimating the level of *bridging* social capital generated by the voluntary and community sectors. Close inspection shows that many of the organizations that form the voluntary sector are bonded by specific interests, whether based on ethnicity, health interests, disability or age, or else they are agencies run by salaried staff supported by a small group of volunteers that form a management committee. The social capital that is generated by the voluntary sector may be less than anticipated and is still likely to be in the form of bonding rather than bridging social capital.

The professionally run and delivered welfare provision and public services may be blamed for the loss of reciprocal neighbourliness, but there are other factors that also have to be taken into account. In particular, the loss of the daytime availability of women as employment has become the norm. Traditionally it has been women who have been the ones with the capacity for generalized, reciprocal behaviour. Furthermore, the health of market economies depends on the ascendancy and predominance of self-pleasing individuals, and this cultural value is not conducive to generalized reciprocity. One suspects that to focus on these factors would involve breaching political correctness as well as questioning the virtues of capitalist systems which governments on both sides of the Atlantic are loathe to do and for this reason are restricting themselves to tinkering with the way in which public services are delivered. So, no longer are vast numbers of workers employed by public bodies to 'do things' for people. Instead, local people, despite the shortened radius of social trust in their neighbourhood, are being coaxed into active involvement in shaping and even running the public services in their neighbourhood. Not only does this involve labouring in contexts of chronic distrust, they also have to do this from a position of relative powerlessness, especially in comparison with the professionally trained and salaried staff of the budget-holding public bodies.

Efforts to equip local people to embark upon more active participation in the services provided within their community is referred to as *capacity building*. However, such efforts so far have been quite feeble in relation to the immensity of the challenge imposed upon local people in poor communities. Much capacity building revolves around local people visiting other communities to see what they have achieved, learning the responsibilities of management committees and producing a community newsletter. For those who are elected to positions of responsibility the training becomes more specific, for example covering issues such as how to chair meetings, how to conduct interviews for the appointment of staff and preparing presentations and public speaking. So far the commitment to capacity building has been short term and unimaginative and in the hands of those who clearly benefit from tutoring and mentoring local people.[7] In many poor neighbourhoods, residents perceive disproportionate benefits[8] accruing to 'the men in suits' and this provokes cynicism in people, and cynicism undermines social capital as much as fear. In these contexts where hope gets rapidly contaminated by cynicism, those committed to the regeneration of social capital might find it instructive to review the quiet work undertaken by local churches and individual Christians in both Britain and the USA.

Churches: unsurpassed generators of bridging social capital

In the British context, the commitment to bridging social capital has been expressed through the age-old notion of 'parish'. The Church of England, as the established Church, extends its commitment to those beyond the congregation. This inclusive approach that embraces everyone within a particular geographic area was once motivated by the Church's covert function of maintaining social control. Freed from this potent function, and more fragile than ever before, the temptation is to conclude that the parish structure is an anachronism. The new understanding of the value and sparcity of examples of bridging social capital may prompt a fuller evaluation of the parish system before it is considered to be financially unsustainable and terminally unfashionable.

The contemporary relevance of 'parish' is well illustrated in this example from the Isle of Dogs:

The Isle of Dogs once had the unwelcome status of being the one locality in Britain to have elected a candidate from the British National Party to political office.[9] Despite a relatively high turnout for a by-election for ward councillor (42 per cent) the BNP candidate won by seven votes. Derek Beackon of the BNP became the councillor for the Millwall ward where almost 30 per cent of the ward population was Bangladeshi. The ward boundary and the boundary of the Anglican parish was virtually the same.

It was clear that campaigning needed to be focused rapidly if Derek Beackon was to be ousted in the May elections. The worry was that he would be re-elected with an increased majority since he had tapped into a genuine seam of resentment based on the perception that the Bangladeshi community was receiving better housing than the longstanding, indigenous community. The immense upheaval and re-shaping of the locality, through the construction and cre-ation of the phenomenon of 'Docklands' and Canary Wharf, also played a part, but the grievances this prompted were less easy to articulate than the grievances against Bangladeshi residents.

The churches worked hard to counteract the increasing permission being given to talk and act in racist ways. The speed of response by the churches was helped by the long-established weekly ecumenical prayer meeting, and this provided a foundation that enabled the churches to move promptly and purposefully, so too did the fact of their long-term presence in the community. However, the group of church leaders had to face the fact that some church members were supportive of the BNP's arguments and that contact with Bangladeshi residents was limited, mainly through the church school, a neighbourhood advice centre run by the United Reformed Church and a youth project in the neighbourhood. Nevertheless, the churches' depth of knowledge of the community proved to be more robust and extensive than that of other agencies. Contact with the Bengali community had also been enhanced by the commitment of the parish team to maintain a disciple of visiting the sick and wherever possible to welcome newcomers to the neighbourhood - including Bangladeshis. Little did they know that six years later they would find themselves needing to draw on this expression of bridging social capital. Nor did the members of the ecumenical prayer group realise that their quiet commitment[10] to praying together would provide the foundation for working together in the midst of emotional and political agitation.

Even though the churches felt that their contact was superficial and limited to the leaders of the Bengali community they were very aware that the only hope in this context would be to find ways in which people from the two communities could get to know each and so lessen resentment. And this, combined with more accurate information about how public resources were allocated, especially in relation to housing, might serve to counteract the arguments being put by the BNP.[11]

After the election of Derek Beackon as the BNP local councillor, therefore, the vicar and other church leaders worked with the leading members of the Bengali community to extend invitations to both the indigenous, long-standing white residents and Bangladeshi residents to a party in the church hall on the first Sunday in the New Year. People were invited to bring food to share, and the invitation was to all the members of the family. From the Bengali community 40 people came, mostly men and children.

During the party everyone was invited to stand on a giant map of the Isle of Dogs.[12] The challenge was to locate the place where you lived – and then to say hello and discover your neighbours. In the corner of the room people were able to do simple origami. By the time the party had ended everyone was the proud owner of a neatly folded and brightly coloured paper flower. The significance of the origami shapes could not have been anticipated. Over the following days people placed the origami shapes on their window ledges. They became a shared symbol that that household recognized and valued a wider community in the Isle of Dogs than just their own kind. Bridging social capital had been created.

As the May election drew closer the churches invited their members, as well as others, to wear rainbow ribbons on their lapel. The aim was to help people make a positive statement about where they stood as well as to give the message that there were lots of people who would not be voting BNP. To ensure that people were protected from the fear of intimidation escorts as well as transport were provided by church members and the Neighbourhood Project run by the United Reformed Church.

When it came to the local election people used the ballot box to reject the BNP.

This real-life situation illustrates the commitment to bridging social capital by the Christian churches, and the capacity of the churches to widen the radius of trust in the neighbourhood. First impressions might suggest that by harnessing hospitality, celebration and creativity the right conditions are created to achieve this. However a more rigorous interrogation of the process provides some important insights into how it is possible to build positive aspects of social capital even in a fraught situation. For example:

♦ Positioning was key – without the trust engendered by the ecumenical prayer group and the commitment to welcoming Bangladeshi householders, it is doubtful if a strategy could have emerged from *within* the community.

♦ Courage, sensitivity and skill were needed to *surface* the aspects of diversity that distressed people. A balance had to be found between enabling people to express their concerns (for this was the secret of Derek Beackon's success), and challenging the misconceptions and wrong assumptions that contributed to the scapegoating of Bangladeshis.

♦ Facts had to be sought about the allocation of housing and these facts had to be presented firmly and regularly, but not aggressively.

♦ Church members had to be empowered to resist and challenge their neighbours when they indulged in racist talk. This was hugely demanding, because in the past they too may have lent their energy to stereotyping and blaming their Bangladeshi neighbours.

♦ Layer upon layer of invitations had to be made via schools, old people's clubs, the pubs, the local shops, the mosques, as well as leafleting every flat and house in the area.

♦ The events to which people were invited had to be characterized by *mutual* activity rather than being reliant on the easier option of providing entertainment – even multicultural entertainment. The aim was to encourage people to participate rather than remain onlookers.

♦ Structures had to be provided which encouraged conversation and dialogue between those who had never spoken to each other before.

♦ The activities that took place at the different events had the aim of identifying and sharing the connections that existed between people, despite their apparent diversity. The 'bondship' of the Isle of Dogs needed to be valued and affirmed: but now that bondship needed to include those who were different – the Bangladeshi community. This widening of the 'bondship' involved helping people to discover connections between each other, such as parents with children in the same class, getting the same newspaper from the same newsagent, sharing the same birthday. These connections already existed, but had been swamped by the dominating perception of difference and threat. The challenge was to generate a 'fusing of horizon and humanity'.[13]

This list highlights the commitment, creativity and sensitivity that are required to build the capacity of local residents to accept the legitimacy of newcomers in the neighbourhood. The fact that churches have been present in a community for decades, if not centuries, counts for something. No other agency will have the voice and depth of history that the Church represents, and the local church must harness, and be *allowed* to harness, this asset wisely and generously because it cannot easily be replicated. It also emphasizes the significance of a long-term commitment to bridging social capital by the churches, without this the churches would neither have been positioned nor have had the credibility to respond to the situation.

In the USA, research has shown how involvement in a church can enable people to 'get ahead' despite having faced long-term, social deprivation. For example, involvement in a religious congregation is the best predictor of gaining employment because it enables the unemployed person to gain access to a network that is alert to employment opportunities. There is also growing evidence of the effectiveness of local churches in counteracting aggressive drug culture in their communities.[14] Speaking of his experience in New York City, community developer Van Johnson believes that there is no substitute for the resources of energy, enthusiasm, political clout and economic pull that churches offer to community developers. To quote Johnson: 'I will never again attempt to help people with economic revitalisation, unless it is under the umbrella of a church. It makes no sense, especially in the black community, to leave the church out. The church is the most important institution we have. It holds most of the resources that our community needs.'[15] US Government funding is now deliberately handed to churches in recognition that the Church, when harnessing Christian teaching and working for individual conversions, may be the key agency in achieving transformation of long-term, distressed communities.

Churches in the USA have achieved an impressive track record in improving the *liveabilty*[16] of neighbourhoods. They now refer to this process as *reneighbouring* the city. They aim to counteract the flight away from inner urban neighbourhoods by those who have the choice.[17] As was noted earlier, Julius Wilson suggests that this movement out of the neighbourhood by long-established, 'respectable' residents can trigger a negative, downward spiral. Reneighbouring involves Christians choosing to live in areas that others are trying to escape from, i.e. areas of extensive and multiple deprivation. This commitment to reneighbouring is also part of the British scene. For example, David and Frances Hawkey, who had previously been missionaries with the Church Mission Society, lived for ten years in Broadwater Farm in north London, having moved to the estate immediately after the riot. They were consistent and supportive neighbours committed to modelling generalized reciprocity. On occasions they were advocates for neighbours faced with injustice, they worked with people from the estate to develop a health centre and they were stalwarts of the annual carnival. Broadwater Farm is now cited as one of the most successfully renewed neighbourhoods. However, regeneration practitioners who have evaluated the process in Broadwater Farm have repeatedly failed to recognize the significant contribution provided by Christians (a Roman Catholic Sister and two African Pastors in addition to the Hawkeys) to increase the radius of social trust between residents of the estate as well as enhance the capacity of local people to engage in the regeneration programme that the local authority initiated. In Wolverhampton, likewise, the contribution of the Hope Community, led by Margaret Walsh, has gone unrecognized by regeneration specialists. On the South Acton estate, households from the Oak Tree Anglican Fellowship have moved into houses affected by planning blight in order to create networks of generalized reciprocity among what risks becoming a community of the 'left-behind'. Urban Expression is yet another network of Christian households committed to living within disadvantaged communities. There are no doubt many more initiatives such as these but they are yet to attract the attention of the growing professional cadre of regeneration experts who, formed by the chilly, secular winds that blow across Britain and northern Europe, rarely have eyes or ears that can perceive the impact of those who take their faith and the gift of fraternal relations seriously.

Brave social capital

In addition to bridging and bonding social capital, I should like to add a third category, that of brave social capital.[18] This category is needed if we are to distinguish between the generalized reciprocity that develops into bridging social capital and the commitment to work for the well-being of those who are not just different, but are perceived as carrying a threat or menace. Such commitment, I believe, should be distinguished from bridging social capital, and warrants the label brave social capital.

Those who are involved in the winter night shelters, if they think about it, could encounter an extensive list of potential threats – violence, TB, HIV/AIDS, head lice, fleas and so on. Those who opt to live on 'hard-to-let' estates face a higher risk of the car being stolen or being broken into, noise and other anti-social behaviour – if they think about it. Nevertheless, despite the potential threats, commitment to brave social capital is more extensive than might be expected. It is often (although certainly not always) people with a religious faith who are willing to make such risky and demanding commitments. The motivation for this might be the desire to achieve a close integration between one's beliefs and one's actions, or it might be the product of a psychological need to 'help and rescue' others. It certainly involves a willingness to stick one's neck out, and for ordinary people, Christians or not, making such a commitment requires some kind of structure to make such a risky contribution possible. For example, it would be foolhardy to open one's house to unknown homeless people on one's own: however, as part of a structure with clear boundaries, responsibilities and manageable tasks allocated on rotas, it becomes possible to contemplate such risky ventures. Structures enable us to journey out to express our fraternal relationship to the most woebegone, menacing, unattractive *and distant*.

When these structures of participation are without power and based on values such as hospitality, concern and kindness, then the expression of brave social capital can unleash the cascade of grace from which an unknowable range of people and situations benefit. This cascade of grace is uncontrollable, unpredictable and virtuous. It speaks of God's Kingdom and gives us a glimpse of what it is to be God's children, and each other's brother and sister. The following story illustrates this widely flowing cascade of grace that is triggered when people opt for brave social capital, and more than this, it highlights how brave social capital can encompass our global context:

> At a Mother's Union meeting in a village in Kent the speakers were three Mother's Union workers from Zimbabwe. In their presentation they spoke of how important hand sewing machines were to the villages in Zimbabwe where there was no electricity. The word went round and soon there were eight old sewing machines retrieved from people's lofts and cellars. However, the Zimbabwean women advised that the only way they could reliably reach the villages would be if they were delivered personally.
>
> The British women, all over 60, were faced with a challenge - would they organize a few jumble sales to pay the shipping costs only to have the machines moulder in a customs yard, or would they go to Zimbabwe themselves and carry the sewing machines to the villages? Would they choose venturesome love[19] or would they opt for what, in theological terms, Bonhoeffer would have described as cheap grace?

They chose the route that characterizes brave social capital, and grace cascaded in the following ways:

- The local newspaper followed the women's story at every stage, carrying the implicit message that church involvement does not have to be dull and predictable.
- The families of the women hotly debated whether their mother was being reckless in taking such risks ... especially with her bad back. The grandchildren, however, thought that their grandmother was *cool*.
- Prayer became passionate.
- An understanding of world development issues grew.
- The women were transformed by their experience - and were radicalized and sensitized by the experience.[20]
- An ongoing relationship was created between villagers in Zimbabwe and villagers in Kent.

These are only the immediate gracious outcomes. There would be more because the potency of the experience would resonate throughout the Kentish women's lives. The cascade of grace is so overflowing it cannot be tracked. Each time the children, grandchildren and even great-grandchildren of these women are confronted by a challenge to express fraternal relations to a stranger they will no doubt reflect on the boldness that is part of their inheritance. And this will change the future for the better.

Notes

1 Francis Fukuyama, *The Great Disruption* (London: Profile Books, 2000).

2 Trustworthiness is essential to capitalism. If trust is lost in companies that invite people to invest in them then our world economic system becomes vulnerable. This is why Enron *et al.* has provoked such a crisis.

3 In very poor communities generalized reciprocity can disintegrate into economic activity as those who are desperately poor seek out opportunities to be helpful – in the hope that a tip might follow.

4 Robert D. Putnam, *Bowling Alone* (New York: Simon and Schuster), 2000, p. 23.

5 Ibid., p. 21.

6 William Julius Wilson, *The Truly Disadvantaged: The Inner City, the Underclass and Public Policy* (Chicago: Chicago University Press, 1988).

7 The Neighbourhood Renewal Unit has recognized the alienating effect on local people when well-paid, professional consultants are the first to benefit from a programme of regeneration or renewal. Therefore, a scheme has been introduced to enable residents to become trainers and capacity builders. This attempt to have a 'medium' that reinforces the 'message' is surely a positive development, and the extent to which such

arrangements gain momentum is an important indicator of the success of the policy of neighbourhood renewal.

8 A strong lobby is being organized to pay local people for their involvement in local management boards and local strategic partnerships because the officers from the statutory agencies involved in these activities are paid for their contribution. This development may score high in terms of fairness but it will further erode the inclination for voluntary commitment.

9 Sadly, at the time of writing the BNP has claimed eight seats in the English local elections. This indicates yet further loss of bridging social capital in local communities.

10 Ecumenical commitment is an expression of bridging social capital.

11 The churches also negotiated with other political parties in Tower Hamlets to ensure that their campaign literature did not pander to the growing anti-Bangladeshi attitudes and that hustings were disciplined. This contract agreed between the political parties in Tower Hamlets was adopted by the Council for Racial Equality in the 2001 general election when party leaders pledged not to permit racist arguments to be used in their campaigns.

12 As regular viewers of 'Eastenders' will know, the Isle of Dogs is not an island but a peninsular in the River Thames, but the impact of Commercial Road at the top of the peninsular makes it feel as if it is an island.

13 This expression was used by Sue Mayo, who worked with the ecumenical group, facilitated through funding from the Joseph Rowntree Foundation. Sue Mayo, a community artist and librettist, was the architect of the participatory events that took place on the Isle of Dogs during this period, and I am indebted to her analysis in relation to the points identified above. For more details of this period in the Isle of Dogs' history, see Nick Holtham and Sue Mayo, *Learning From The Conflict*, A Jubilee Group Pamphlet c/o Ken Leech, St. Botolph's, Aldgate, London EC3N 1AB.

14 See, for example, Robert Carle, 'Church-Based Community Development and the Transformation of New York', *Trinity News* 44(1): 14; LeRoy Gruner, 'Heroin, Hashish, and Hallelujah: The Search for Meaning', *Review of Religious Research* 26(2): 176–84; Carol Steinbach, 'Program Helps Restore Ailing Community', *Progressions* 5(1): 21; Robert D. Carle and Louis D. Decaro (eds) *Signs of Hope in the City* (Valley Forge, PA:, Judson Press, 1999).

15 Quoted in Diane Wilson 'Black Church Expands Communitarian Tradition' *Progressions* 5(1): 7.

16 The term *liveability* is used by government policy-makers to describe how 'at home or at ease' people feel in their neighbourhood. Research has shown that improvements in housing and the physical environment have little effect on the 'liveability' rating unless there is also an increase in the radius of social trust.

17 See Robert D. Lupton, *Return Flight: Community Development Through Reneigboring Our Cities* (Atlanta: FCS Urban Ministries, 1997).

18 Robert Putnam in his study of southern Italy coined the term 'brave reciprocity' to describe the effort and commitment of some to rise above the *amoral familism* that prevails in some parts of Italy (we're talking Mafia here!). See Putnam, R. with Leonardi, R. and Nanetti, R.Y. *Making Democracy Work: Civic Traditions in Modern Italy* (Princeton, NJ: Princeton University Press, 1993).

19 Surely a more poetic term to describe the concept of brave social capital!

20 A much underestimated force in the world is that of a radicalized older woman.

4

The Significance of a
Story-rich Life

Involvement in bridging and brave social capital provides people with a story-rich life and churches need to be adept at harnessing this. For example, the visit to villages in Zimbabwe by the group of older women lugging hand sewing machines would have generated countless stories. Those who made the journey became story-rich in a way that distinguished them from others in their community; the experience shaped their identity. Likewise, those involved in the New Year party on the Isle of Dogs would have found that they gained an additional and probably richer seam of story in their lives. The experience of the party and the other events that took place when the Isle of Dogs was in the media spotlight will have been retold in many situations. One can speculate that it made for an animated conversation during a three-week visit to Canada to see a sister who had left the Isle of Dogs 30 years previously. One can imagine some of the Bangladeshi men retelling their experience to their companions at the Stepney mosque. A story has been created; a story gives a sense of distinctive identity to the teller, a story can travel round the globe and a story can travel across time.

Stories are so much part of our lives that their significance is easily overlooked: often the impact of stories remains invisible and unacknowledged. I share here an example of how an everyday encounter could have created a story that could travel round the world and have had an impact on people from a culture profoundly different from my own.

South London had been subject to the most amazingly heavy and sudden downpours. On my leisurely day off I was determined to be prepared. I opted to wear my expensive waterproof, breathable jacket, with hood, as well as take my golf-size umbrella. The downpours were not going to deter me.

As I got off the bus the heavens opened and I congratulated myself on being well prepared. I put up the large brolly and went on my way, well pleased. As I came to the pedestrian island in the middle of the High Road, I was confronted by three Somali women. Each was dressed in a burka that covered them from head to toe. They didn't have anything to protect them from the rain and they were getting drenched. As I came towards them I smiled and gestured with my 'big enough for three' umbrella, inviting them to take it from me. They smiled back and the encounter became one that spoke of envy of how well prepared I was. In fact, in the brief encounter, the story that flashed through my mind was that of the wise virgins who had thought to bring sufficient oil for their lamps so that they could be prepared even when the bridegroom was delayed.

More than anything I had wanted to give my brolly to those women, but I missed my chance. I only had a split second to express that wish. All I needed was to gesture once more with my hand and move the giant golf umbrella closer to them. But I didn't, I was too slow, and too soon we had moved in opposite directions and the moment was lost.

I was so disappointed. I had blown it, I couldn't bring myself to run back to give them the umbrella, there was too much traffic to do that. For a while I nursed my failure: I had a hood on my coat I could have put on, at home I had another golf brolly (I had bought two at the same time). I was annoyed that my mind had immediately gravitated to an 'I'm alright Jack' story. To add to my dismay I realized that if I had managed to transfer that umbrella into the hands of the Somali women, a story would have been created that might have travelled round the world, and might even have become a story that could heal.

I speculated that when the women arrived home their giant umbrella would have attracted attention. They would have given an account of the brief encounter. Each time the umbrella was taken out in the anticipation of rain, the story of its origin would be recalled. As the Somali household had to cope with abuse and rejection and downright rudeness, they might just remember the moment on that rainy day that was different. There might even be an occasion, many years in the future when the story of the umbrella given by a stranger would be told to youngsters in Somalia, to help widen their perspective on the ways of the world.

Such musings remain a fantasy because I failed to respond in the way I really wanted to. However, I am aware that I can only tell this story because it tells of how I messed up, how I blew it. The story revolves around my failure to act with generosity of spirit. Just as an aside, I have a hunch that my failure is linked to a more significant failure – a failure in relation to prayerfulness. One of the things that prayerfulness brings is timing, timing which enables grace to flow unimpeded. However, God's graciousness is not to be inhibited by my lack of prayerfulness and sluggishness in relation to moving towards strangers. What has resulted is the availability of a story which illustrates the extraordinary capacity of 'story' to travel across cultures and even to travel through time. If I had managed to give that brolly away I would never have been able to share the story publicly for fear of sounding a prig!

Story is like currency in that it can change hands without losing value. The telling of a story hands it over to others, who in turn can tell it to other people. This ability is quite extraordinary. William James suggests that the greatest gap which exists in the universe is that between one human mind and another, yet the potency of stories is such that they are 'Our best hope for flying over the chasms that separate individuals, races, genders, ages (and ages) and the myriad other differences that render us unique (and potentially lonely). ... Flying to other planets is child's play compared to crossing the light years between the galaxy of your mind and the galaxy of mine. Story can be such a time traveller'.[1]

The stories we are party to also shape our identities *and* inform some of the choices we make. This potency of stories is essential to holistic mission. By enabling people to achieve a story-rich life an oblique route is found by which to influence their values, shape their character and inform the priorities and decisions they make in the future. Involvement in the struggle for the Kingdom of God brings with it a story-rich rich life and this opens an oblique route that links action for the Kingdom of God and ultimately opens up to people the possibility of seeing and accepting the significance of Jesus in our lives.

Each of us will have stories and events in our lives that carry a special significance and their influence is more extensive than is recognized. For example, Taylor speaks of his conviction that 'Stories go somewhere to roost, somewhere deep inside our spirits. They settle there, beyond consciousness, to grow, blend with other stories and experiences, and work their influence from below, subject only to the distant call of memory.'[2] When I first read this assesment by Taylor I thought it was a rather extravagant claim. It made me scrutinize my own life because I was reluctant to accept that the choices I may have made in my life were the product of such unacknowledged and imperceptible forces. As I did this I recalled an experience I had when I was a youngster:

My Mum was a shop assistant, working mostly in a small newsagent and tobacconist shop, or what as a child I called a 'sweet shop'. Each day after school I would go to the shop and linger in the hope that a packet of crisps or a lucky bag would be noted on my Mum's bill and passed into my nine-year-old hand. On one occasion, my Mum called me over and gave me six packets of cigarettes.[3] 'Please take these to the caravans and give them to Mrs Doherty. She left them in the shop and she will be wondering where they are.' I protested, 'But,

Mum, they're gypsies.' She replied very straightforwardly, 'Yes they are gypsies, and they are very good customers.'

I went off rather reluctantly to the site that had once been covered by 'prefabs' but had been home to twenty gypsy caravans for the past six months. In my mind, I thought it odd that my Mum was sending me to the gypsies while all my friends' mothers insisted that on no account must they go near the gypsy site. I also wondered how I was to find Mrs Doherty, cross that my mother hadn't thought about that. However, I needn't have worried. As soon as I entered the bounds of the camp carrying the cigarettes Mrs Doherty ran to greet me. She was so pleased and so grateful, and insistent that I carry her thanks to my mother for going to such trouble. I felt proud of my Mum, I rather liked Mrs Doherty and I rather liked the fact that I could boast to my friends that me and my Mum were friends of Mrs Doherty on the gypsy site.

Twenty years later I found myself calling together the handful of people who had dared to write letters to the local newspaper expressing a different view from the venomous and abusive letters that dominated the letters page each time the travellers moved into town. Together we formed a liaison group with the gypsies, endeavouring to improve communication between them and their angry, house-dwelling neighbours. We successfully lobbied for a teacher to work with the children, and for support from health visitors. It was rewarding but demanding voluntary work and I often wondered why I had ever got involved...

I now endorse Taylor's observation that story 'does its work from below'. I had never associated the encounter with Mrs Doherty, prompted by my Mum, with the unusual and often mocked voluntary work I took on two decades later. Taylor goes on to write, 'Our essential orientation to life is a consequence of the stories that form us. A genuine story will not leave us alone. It insists, sometimes in the most impolite terms, on changing us.'[4] The churches' winter night shelters have proved to be a source of transforming stories, and not just for those with direct involvement. I remember Gwen, one of the key volunteers at one of the participating churches, telling me how her granddaughter was bemused by all the homeless men who knew her by name when they went out shopping. I visualized it like this:

Gwen had her granddaughter staying with her for half term. Together they went to the nearby street market. In addition to bumping into neighbours and friends in the market, Gwen was also stopped by the three men sitting on the bench, with cans of Special Brew at their feet. They called to her by name, and she introduced her granddaughter to them, introducing each of them by name to her. She asked about their health and where they were living and they in turn asked about her, and whether the church hall would be opening again during the winter.

In the cafe at the table by the door sat an unkempt figure with a long-cold cup of tea. When Gwen and her grand-daughter entered, his face lit up and he shouted a fulsome hello to Gwen, which she happily returned, calling him by name. As Gwen and her granddaughter drank their coffee and ate their toast, the granddaughter ventured to ask how her Gran knew all these alcoholics and mad men. Gwen told her about the winter night shelter that she helped with, and she went on to tell her granddaughter how Bill, sitting in the corner over there, would sit with *The Times* crossword and could complete it in twenty minutes, and Pete, whom she had chatted with, had been a soldier who fought in the Falklands and how he always helped her put the camp beds away and swept the hall for her.

First reaction to this might be to be pleased that the reputation of the Church had been enhanced in the eyes of a young person. Here was an example the granddaughter might hold on to that spoke of the relevance and commitment of a local church. Perhaps it might lead her to speak up for the Church when she heard people bemoaning that it was made of money or full of child molesters. But this would only be the superficial impact of the episode. The example that her Gran gave her of being alongside those whom others disparaged, and her commitment to have a go despite the cynicism of others, would have an impact on that young woman for the rest of her life. It would inform the decisions she would make from then on.[5] Her decisions would be less likely either to be governed by her own comfort and self interest or to be shaped by the self-centred mores of the wider society. Her choices, consciously or unconsciously, would be closer to those that serve the Kingdom of God.

Generative stories and an oblique approach to mission

Taylor provides a tentative definition of 'story'. He suggests that 'A story is the telling of the significant actions of characters over time'.[6] However, some stories have a particular potency and these I wish to describe as *generative* stories. Generative stories are characterized by:

♦ being specific to the person,[7] i.e. they speak of a person's unique encounter or pattern of encounters;
♦ having the capacity to become a building block of a person's identity;
♦ combining the themes of both hope and struggle;
♦ carrying an imperative to make some kind of response, either consciously or, as Taylor suggests, doing their work from below, unseen and acknowledged;
♦ carrying an emotional potency that provokes an internal conversation as the person endeavours to integrate the experience into their value system.

Generative stories are the often unacknowledged but potent events that help to make people different. They are an underestimated aspect of the nature/nurture debate that underpins much of our social scientific analysis. Family, schooling and social class have all been acknowledged as shaping who we are, but on a micro-level it is the stories that enter our lives which also play a part, for good or ill, in the shape that each of our futures will take.

For example, the women who carried sewing machines to villages in Zimbabwe will continue to express exceptional commitment to Zimbabwe. No doubt they will find themselves being able to speak with 'attitude' when others pass comment on the political situation in the country. Some of the people who attended that New Year party on the Isle of Dogs will have absorbed it as one of the defining stories in their lives. They will be the ones who are most alert to the eruption of racist sentiment in the community in the future. Both groups have been party to a story that shapes them and informs the decisions and action they will take in the future. Furthermore, in these two instances, the people involved in the events have become sensitized to kingdom or justice issues in a way that no amount of preaching and cajoling could have achieved.

My thesis is that by enabling people to develop a story-rich life, i.e. a life characterized by positive, generative stories, then we equip them to:

♦ understand the Gospel more fully;
♦ respond to the invitation of Jesus to develop 'fraternal relations' with those outside our usual network of friends and family.

There is, however, an indication of a third, gracious outcome: that those in their third age with lives rich in generative stories can have a positive influence, particularly on young people, to the extent of informing the decisions that they go on to make in their future lives.

The vocation of age?

There is a growing amount of evidence to support the idea that older people have a special capacity to shape positively the lives of the next-but-one generation. For example, the research of Minkler and Roe[8] highlights the significance of grandparents in the choices that their grandchildren make. They researched the life histories of children addicted to crack-cocaine in Harlem, New York. They concluded that one of the best predictors of the young person being able to get free of their addiction was the level of involvement of their grandmother in their lives. The more involved their grandmother was, the more likely they were to rise above their addiction.

On a larger canvas, Bob Martin, a zoologist based at the University of Zurich, has reflected on the *strange* phenomenon of menopause in *Homo sapiens* and the large sea mammals. According to Martin, the females of all species, with the exception of *Homo sapiens* and the large sea mammals, do not survive much beyond menopause. This, he suggests, fits with the accepted view of evolutionary biology: that the procreation of the next generation is the prime goal of all species. The biological norm is that once the female becomes barren her contribution to the species is over and the unforgiving dynamic of evolution decrees that her life is redundant. Martin suggests that a different pattern has emerged in the 'advanced' species of *Homo sapiens* and the large marine mammals. Because their (our) social environment is so complex the parenting generation alone is unable to adequately socialize their offspring. Thus the contribution of the grandparenting generation to the effective nurture and shaping of the offspring is so significant that these species, in evolutionary terms, have invested in the older, barren, 'wise' female.

The ability of older people to shape the future actions of the next-but-one generation can be partly explained by the research of cognitive psychologists. Piaget is possibly the best-known psychologist concerned with the way in which we think and perceive. Even today, almost a century after he conducted his research, the observations that Piaget made of the different thinking styles of toddlers, children and young people remain the backbone of the cognitive psychology taught to student teachers. Piaget noted how thinking styles develop according to age. However, he and the vast majority of those who have followed in his footsteps have assumed that the pinnacle of thinking styles is *formal* logic which most people achieve by the age of seventeen or eighteen.

Formal logic involves being able to analyse the range of factors acting on a situation in order to reach a right answer. Formal logic can obviously be applied to mathematical puzzles, but some occupations rely extensively on this capacity for diagnostic thinking. The bank counter clerk will, at the end of the day, make a series of calculations using the records of transactions he or she has made in order to track down how it is that there is a £20 error. The computer engineer will spend hours trying different options in order to exclude particular faults from the frame. Medical doctors apply formal logic unceasingly, so too do scientific researchers. Our society values formal logic very highly, and the more adept the practitioner needs to be at arriving at a correct answer the more likely they are to be highly rewarded.

But formal logic is not the end of the story as Piaget suggested. Klaus Riegal, also a cognitive psychologist, suggests that as adults we have the capacity for *dialectical logic*.[9] Dialectical logic ends up with a question rather than an answer. It requires the capacity to tolerate contradictions and incomplete information. Dialectical logic is more concerned with posing more profound questions than it is with arriving at a right answer. Dialectical logic respects the fact that life is too complicated and rich to be encapsulated within our thinking. However, this awareness, instead of disappointing and closing down our thinking, entices, teases and energizes the thinking process.[10]

My hunch is that one of the significant contributions of older people to the socialization of the next-but-one generation is to enable them to glimpse the richness and relevance of dialectical logic. In contrast, the parenting generation is likely to be fixated with enhancing their child's capacity for formal logic. Parents want their child to get as many right answers as possible, and know right from wrong as clearly as it can distinguish between black and white. Yet, the child knows deep within them that there is more to life than this, and furthermore the child wants to discover right and wrong not by being told but by exploration.

I did not get to know any of my grandparents but my life was graced by my rather elderly Auntie Carrie. Even now, I can rekindle the times in my early teens, when I would take myself to her house, just a hundred yards away, and talk about nothing in particular. With hindsight I recognize how she provided me with a wider perspective on life. She could subtly rebuke me without causing offence - quite an art with volatile teenagers.

She laughingly suggested that I had 'promises like piecrust', as I repeated yet again a rash promise to paint a cupboard for her. It took me ten days to ponder what the expression meant, and when I had realized, I found myself having to agree with her. To counteract my inclination to accuse others of some injustice or blame others for their inadequacies, she would sigh, 'Ah well, the man who is perfect is yet to be born ... and his mother is dead'. With hindsight, this was a kind of Advent longing. Auntie Carrie also prompted the first stirrings of compassion within me. When the media pilloried someone, or when I joined in the hue and cry that someone was a 'no-mark' - the Liverpudlian equivalent of calling someone a wastrel - she would add the coda, 'He's some mother's son'.

Auntie Carrie had lived a story-rich life. It was her stories that attracted me to pop in of an evening to see her rather than sit as a couch potato, or go in search of a friend and sit on the wall under the street lamp. Her story-rich life was about simple pleasures in the midst of hardships: providing strangers with a bed for a few nights as they struggled to get their wits together during wartime pressures; being bombed out during the 1941 May blitz; and how her loving husband had been killed because he sat on the cellar steps, instead of right down in the cellar during the air raid. She had stories to share that never seemed to grow stale. And as Taylor comments, 'Stories, like mother's milk, are filled with nutrients from which lives grow'.[11] It was Auntie Carrie, more than anyone, who provided me with the stories and the corrections that somehow could never have been provided by parents or friends.

Martha Nussbaum observes that the stories that a child

hears and learns provide a pervasive and powerful way of learning its society's values and structures.[12] I am aware, even as I write now, of the impact of Auntie Carrie's story about being bombed out: the fact that Uncle Len lost his life by sitting on the stairs, and hadn't obeyed the standard instruction to go down into the cellar, has influenced my inclination towards obedience rather than disobedience. Taylor, observing how stories have shaped some of the choices he has made in his life, comments that reading *Lord of the Rings* influenced his decision to operate on the side of good. He writes, 'I still do not think such a conviction, rising from an encounter with such a story, has been without consequences. If the change in direction was small at the time, it may have been one that, like a small, early course correction in a planetary probe, has made a larger difference in where I am many years later'.[13]

Taking account of a new map of life

Never before in human history have so many people been able to anticipate longevity beyond a third age and into a fourth age. Peter Laslett, in his book, *A Fresh Map of Life*,[14] highlights this extraordinary development. In all other periods of human history, those who lived into their third age would have been in the minority, especially if they belonged to the mass of poor people. It has only been for the last 50 years that the vast majority of people, regardless of social class, have been able to anticipate a long old age. Laslett suggests that our imagination and expectations are ill-prepared for this sudden development, so response to the opportunities that now present themselves has been slow.

This new map of life has four rather than three stages. The first phase of life is characterized by socialisation, as the child and young adult are coached in the values and lifestyle of mainstream society. The second phase is characterized by household generativity, where in adulthood the person forms their own household and nurtures their children.[15] The third phase is now profoundly different from what it has been hitherto. No longer is the third age to do with relinquishing, or letting go, of one's capacities in the face of the assaults of old age. The task of the third age has been, throughout human history, that of adjusting to the limits imposed by the loss of physical and, possibly, mental prowess. Laslett suggests that in the new map of life this task of relinquishing belongs to the fourth age, which on average lasts for a period of only four years. If the fourth phase of life is characterized by relinquishing, what is the focus of this third age?

The emergence of the third age which can easily last for twenty years has been quite spectacular. However, within our culture there is no sense of the *telos*, or purpose, of this extended third age. Even the media are unsure how to depict the third age. On the one hand, it is presented as a time of sulky tribulation, as characterized by 'One Foot in the Grave'; on the other hand, it is depicted as a second adolescence. The American sit-com 'The Golden Girls' represents the third age as holding all the opportunities of adolescence and none of the disadvantages.

Intuitively, one senses that to have lived a life rich in generative stories brings with it psychological and spiritual resources relevant to both the third and fourth stages of our lives. However, most of us occupy a story-*thin* environment, relying on money splurge occasions such as holidays or treats to punctuate the routine and provide insubstantial rather than generative stories. Not only are third and fourth agers at risk of having lived story-thin lives, the individualistic and market-dominated view of the good life emphasizes how we feel and how we are seen. This is a debilitating pressure for those in their third and fourth ages. Unsurprisingly, therefore, the market for plastic surgery and age-defying potions has become today's alchemy. However, as in the past, all that is discovered or created is fool's gold.

The Church has scarcely begun to respond to this blossoming of older people or to appreciate the scope for harnessing this gift on behalf of the Kingdom of God. It is vital that a focus is proffered which is more profound than just pleasure seeking and taking life easy. This is especially the case if the ability to cope with the demands of the fourth age, and death itself, is to be fostered. It is here where the significance of the stories, that have coalesced to make up one's identity, come into their own. There is an urgent challenge facing the Church to offer vision and leadership in relation to the *telos* for the third age, and in particular we need to emphasize the centrality of *how* we act and *what* we are, as being the enduring touchstones for a third age that equip us to cope with the formidable tasks that face us in our fourth age.

Stories: the backbone of our morality

How we act and what we are is a good description of morality, and stories are the foundation of morality. The stories that form us incline us to respond in one way rather than another. Stories provide a basis for ethical behaviour much more potently than reason, because stories engage with all aspects of the person, and in particular they engage the emotions. We *experience* a story, and experiences shape us in a way that abstractions cannot. Taylor writes that, 'Story acts by incarnation, giving flesh and life to what is otherwise detached and abstract'.[16] The knowledge that we gain through a story is concrete and specific, and often it is the messy particulars that enrich a story. In contrast, rationality tends to sidestep the messy particulars because rationality seeks out and promotes universal principles and theories, which are then to be applied to specific situations.[17]

The stories that surround us are the components of day-to-day morality. In our society we may be intellectually preoccupied with the relativism associated with a fragmented post-modern culture, but in our bones, and even in our hearts we remain drawn by the microdramas of 'ought' and 'should' that are played out in the stories to which we are party. Taylor suggests that 'Stories ask for understanding. ... Stories tend to make us more tolerant and forgiving of moral failure at the same time that they convince us of the reality and necessity of the moral dimension of life. A person steeped in stories is less likely to be judgemental, but more likely to realize that judgements must be made'.[18]

> I grew up in a household where money was sometimes short. This meant desperation after one had smoked the last cigarette in the pack. My father was in the midst of such a crisis, and resorted to using a foreign coin to get cigarettes from a cigarette machine. Twenty-four hours later, after getting his pay packet, he went back to the shop and apologized for his mistake, and handed over legal tender in lieu of the foreign coin he had put in the machine.

This example from my father has shaped my attitude. It means that, for me, misdemeanours need to be put in a context before they are judged, and that whenever possible one should make every effort to put things right. To have been party to the first part of the story, using a foreign coin, and not making efforts to put it right, would have given a different message that would have been equally potent to the young hearer. Here we have the nuts and bolts of Paul's urging in his letter to the Romans: that we heed the impact that our actions can have on our weaker brother.[19]

Stories, however, carry another dynamic that goes to the intimate core of who we are. Most of us can rise no higher than the stories that surround us, for the stories with which we grow up inform our imagination and compose our world. The capacity to see ourselves as something more and better than we presently are is dependent on the stories that we encounter, for in our imagination we continually link the past and the present with the future. We find our 'potential self' in the stories that surround us; however, these stories are likely to be both good and bad and therefore if stories have any power at all, they have the power for both good and ill.

Wounded memories: people and places

The Bulger case shocked the whole nation. Few could understand how two young boys could find within them the urge to take away a young toddler and to murder him brutally. It was rumoured that the two youngsters, the night before their gruesome actions, had both watched the adult video 'Chuckie'. In murdering the toddler they had acted out the story line. It also emerged that one of the youngsters had been surrounded by negative and destructive stories throughout his short life.

My heart goes out to all involved in the Bulger tragedy and to the community of Bootle where it took place. Bootle is where I grew up. It is the place where the personal stories that I have recounted took place. Bootle is a bit like Nazareth, a place from which no one expects good to come. It is clear that stories can have an impact that can carry through time, and it is important to note that the power of stories, just like any potent force, can be for either good or ill. Charles Elliot, in his book *Memory and Salvation*, distinguishes between the loser's memory and the winner's memory. The consequences of whether one holds to a winner's or loser's memory are profound.[20] In Bootle, as well as in other chronically poor communities, there is an inclination to hold on to a loser's memory, because the stories that people encounter are often about losing. And the loser's memory can be expressed corporately and not just by the individual. It is this dynamic which is at the heart of Russ Parker's ministry of healing wounded history.

Parker suggests that both personal and communal memories have three aspects: story, conclusion and consequence. From our stories we draw conclusions about ourselves and such conclusions will have consequences. The memories that we hold on to provide what Parker refers to as 'the map of our hearts', and these memories, and wounded memories in particular, have a shaping influence not just on individuals but on communities and places.[21] There are degenerative or corrosive stories just as there are generative stories, and degenerative stories also have consequences. Facts alone do nothing to counteract degenerative or distorted stories. The only check on negative stories is to counter them with other, more positive stories. Taylor comments that, 'You cannot generally argue individuals or societies out of their story, destructive though it may be, unless there is a better one to replace it.'[22]

For the beaten-down of today, and of history, the stories that they accumulate can be devoid of hope, or contaminated by cynicism. Brueggermann notes that, 'The killing of a hope filled future renders (displaced) people powerless and easy to administer.'[23] As Christians we have to cry out in protest at the stifling of hope. We also have to act. However, if the actions we take are dominated by the idea of meeting people's needs this can obscure the scope for enabling people to embrace generative rather than degenerative stories. For most people, thinking and deciding involves weighing up and sifting the different stories gathered from different people. For those inflicted with a loser's memory, the challenge is to enable that person to encounter generative stories that speak of both hope and struggle and carry an imperative towards some positive action.

Faulty or incomplete stories are also at the root of stereotyping or prejudice:

> I spent some time as a volunteer at a centre for homeless people. My task along with three or four other people was to help distribute clothing. With a couple of trestle tables in front of us and rack after rack of second-hand shirts, jackets and sweaters, the guys would come, a couple at a time, to get what they most needed. It was a pretty soul-destroying task as the quality of the stuff we handed out was pretty grim, with only the occasional star item.
>
> We started to get asylum seekers queuing up with the street homeless and the attitude of those of us 'doing the clothes' changed. We became protective of the shoddy clothes. ... 'These clothes are for homeless people who have to sleep in

the clothes they have on their backs ...'; 'These asylum seekers have got mobile phones ...'; 'Look at his watch ...'; 'Did you see his shoes? ... Crocodile skin'; 'They are only after what they can get ...'; 'They seem to think that we owe them something .... Don't they realize we are volunteers? ...'; 'This is all voluntary you know! ...'.

We were thinking in stereotypes and we were actively reinforcing each other's stereotyping and prejudice. I fear we may even have spread stories about grasping asylum seekers taking the clothes off the backs of (our) homeless people. No doubt, at some stage, we would have succumbed to the temptation of dealing out such a degenerative tale. You have to be tough to resist the temptation to feed other people's prejudices. Only years later have I come to appreciate the destructiveness that is wrought by reinforcing prejudice by trading in incomplete or faulty stories.

This story is pivotal for a number of reasons:

♦ it highlights how involvement in community ministry does not protect us from dealing in faulty, prejudicial stories;
♦ it highlights how apparently authoritative stories can be casually generated;
♦ it highlights the seductive dynamic associated with transmitting 'evidence' that confirms or reinforces another's perspective.

Fact upon fact and statistic upon statistic are not sufficient to shift the majority of us from a prejudicial stance. What is needed are more stories drawn from people with wider experience. Only another story can come alongside a prejudicial story and begin to melt a hardened, convinced heart. The best antidote to incomplete or faulty stories is more stories from different tellers. For those of us working as volunteers at the day centre for homeless people there would have been plenty of stories that could have provided an alternative perspective. The challenge for those managing such a centre is to ensure that staff and volunteers alike are party to stories from a variety of perspectives. Unfortunately, the ways of the world are such that degenerative or destructive stories are circulated with greater ease than the ones that speak of hope and struggle. Hearts can be so hardened that genuine stories of vulnerability and hardship cannot be heard. As Jesus himself often commented, people have to have 'ears to hear'.

According to Taylor, 'A story is indestructible unless the ones who embrace the story chose to destroy it. This is true in the reputedly objective world of science as well as in the overwhelming subjective world of personal relationships. Scientists and feuding couples alike, reveal their humanity in selectively choosing and shaping their facts, often unconsciously, to fit a pre-existing story of how things are.'[24] New information, in whatever form it may take, is often resisted when it confounds settled assumptions and prejudices. This highlights the need for training and reflection to be part of the package provided by the community ministry initiative, or any initiative likely to result in potent stories. If community ministry initiatives and other initiatives that invite people to journey out to encounter the stranger are to challenge stereotyping and prejudice and not feed them, it is vitally important that the following precautions are in place:

♦ volunteers/participants are encouraged to be open to, and to expect, insights that will challenge their assumptions;
♦ debriefing is a regular feature of the volunteers' or participants' experience;
♦ opportunities are provided to reflect on instances that have disturbed or provoked negativity;
♦ those supporting the volunteers or participants are alert to the possibility of stories being created that feed prejudice;
♦ those who support volunteers, and the management committee of the initiative, take seriously their responsibility for promoting reflection at all levels and for all stakeholders;

♦ the importance of encouraging people to make links between their specific experiences and more universal situations is both recognized and implemented.

In the example above I and my fellow volunteers failed to see that grabbing and grasping behaviour didn't just belong to asylum seekers. Their offensive behaviour in this specific instance is behaviour that belongs to humankind. They were manifesting a universal dynamic. If we volunteers had been challenged to reflect more deeply on our experience we may have found ourselves concluding that the asylum seekers were not alone in falling prey to such a temptation. Similar unattractive behaviour has been known to characterize Harrods' sale.

Part of the potency of stories is that they transform inert facts into flesh-and-blood remembrances. Until facts have been interpreted and integrated into some kind of narrative they remain static and powerless. For example, the parents of Stephen Lawrence convinced a Sunday newspaper that there was a deeply dismaying story associated with their son's death. Until then, his murder had been considered to be just one of the many violent deaths that are inflicted on young men in urban areas. The story that the Lawrences told was powerful because the facts surrounding Stephen's death were integrated into a narrative. The events of that night and the days that followed were transformed from mere chrono- logical facts into a pattern that carried meaning and significance. Sir William Macpherson's report on the murder and the actions and inactions of the police highlighted the dynamic of institutional racism[25] clearly for the first time to the British public. It was the *story* of Stephen's death that led to a reshaping of police procedures, and their approach to the Black community. Facts, although available, would not on their own, have been able to carry such power.

Character not just personality

The cult of personality abounds. To have personality is to be a star – or at least to have star potential. However, the high value given to personality is a recent development. Before this preoccupation with personality, what would have mattered most was one's *character*. Taylor suggests that 'Character is a bundle of values in action. . . . In making their choices, characters reveal who they are. They define themselves by the values they live by, often unconsciously.'[26] In a world where personality, i.e. vitality and disposition without values, is lauded, the encounter with generative stories can be subversive. Involvement in community ministry or journeying out to encounter those who are different from us is a means of developing character. Encounters with those who know deeply about struggle are transformational, they rarely leave us unmoved or untouched. Involvement in a local, or even more distant, struggle will likely reveal to each of us a deeper strand or level of our own humanity. This next example illustrates the emergence of character that comes from an encounter with those who would otherwise be distant from us. It too is a story that illustrates the significance of intergenerational encounters.

Pat had been one of the 'movers and shakers' in relation to the local Council of Churches initiative to support frail, elderly people. The manager of the home-care aide service had asked whether the churches could compile a rota of helpers who would provide meals on bank holidays. The scheme started with Christmas Day and Boxing Day, closely followed by New Year's Day. Over this period, Pat had started to get to know Vera, the old lady to whom she had been assigned. Vera was friendly and easy to talk to. On Boxing Day, Karen, Pat's daughter, came with her to meet Vera, and on New Year's Day, it was Karen who went round to collect the plates that had carried the midday meal.

Karen and her Mum didn't see eye to eye on everything. In particular they were at odds with each other over Karen's boyfriend. Karen wanted to get engaged to Pete who worked in a health-food shop. They had been going out together for eighteen months and they wanted to be an item when Karen went off to teacher-training college. Pat felt that they were rushing things.

One of the unexpected gains of the modest initiative set up between Social Services and the Council of Churches was that the focus became as much about friendship as it did about providing meals.[27] In the small market town, popping in to see the housebound person became the norm. Only the hardest of hard-hearted people could have gone from New Year to Easter without calling in for a chat or to check whether any shopping was needed. It wasn't just Pat who called in on Vera in this way, so too did Karen and Pete.

Pat kept checking with Vera that Karen and Pete were not making a nuisance of themselves. Vera reassured her that they were not. Vera told how the three of them would talk about the olden days, and she would tell them how Jack, her husband, used to ride fifteen miles on his bike to see her when they were courting. She told them how she had to sew to prepare her bottom drawer before their marriage. She had shown them the Egyptian cotton pillowslips she had embroidered. In fact, she said they were to have them when she died, before the house-clearers came in and piled everything into a skip.

Vera died that summer and Pat went to her funeral. So too did Karen and Pete, sitting together, near the front of the crematorium. During the short funeral service Pat's mind kept drifting to her daughter and Pete, standing a few rows in front of her. Strangely, they didn't seem quite so young and naive anymore. Somehow, their friendship with Vera, through her last months, and being alongside her as she moved closer to death, had given them character and strength. Pat reflected that having shared together the death of an old lady, possibly they had the character and commitment to share much more. From then on Pat was able to give Karen and Pete a break and get off their backs.

An overview

The aim of this chapter has been to highlight the significance of encouraging people to develop a story-rich life to the missionary task of the Church. Enabling people to achieve a story-rich life provides a novel and oblique route which serves to heighten our inclination towards moral behaviour, *and* set in train a host of other graceful outcomes.

One of the characteristics of generative stories is that they combine the themes of both hope and struggle. Such stories do their work from below, over time influencing the choices a person makes in their life. Generative stories not only remain robust through time, they can also travel across cultures.

The novel demographic pattern in Western nations, where for the first time in human history older people are in the majority, is something that the Church needs to take more seriously. This new map of life provides the Church with a fresh agenda. Active discipleship enables older people to achieve a life rich in generative stories. When a story-rich life is combined with the capacity for dialectical logic the ability to graciously moralize the next-but-one generation becomes a real possibility. This is not a naive assertion; it is based on evidence from the evolutionary journey of *Homo sapiens*.

Stories have power for both good and ill. Both individuals and communities can be caught up in degenerative or corrosive stories. The stories that we are surrounded by will influence our vision of what is possible, as well as the choices we make in our lives. For this reason communities as well as individuals are vulnerable to negative stories that can drag them down. In such contexts, new stories need to be fostered and the wounds made by destructive stories need to be healed.

The accumulation of stories from a single perspective can generate prejudice and stereotyping. This can be a danger in relation to our efforts at journeying out. For this reason initiatives that encourage an encounter with strangers must adopt clear processes to ensure that alternative perspectives and stories are available. Despite this danger of feeding pre-existing prejudices, involvement in community ministry, both locally and internationally, is a sure route for developing character, i.e. a consistent assemblage of values that are expressed in the choices and actions that a person makes.

This business of stories and their capacity to influence the choices we make in our lives is a pivotal concept in this book. My aim is to demonstrate the mission potential of such an approach. This capacity for story to shape people's lives in the direction of the Kingdom of God and of Jesus needs to be taken seriously because it addresses so many of our hopes and fears in relation to mission in a post-modern context. By adopting this oblique route to mission, i.e. promoting opportunities that are likely to be a source of generative stories we find ourselves positioned to:

♦ put into practice a model of holistic mission;
♦ help people to develop a story-rich life at the same time as the wider culture has begun to value a story- or experience-rich life above a materially-rich life;
♦ enable people to express 'fraternal relations' with strangers in accordance with Jesus' life and teaching at a time when bridging social capital is vitally important to people's sense of well-being;
♦ in promoting opportunities for generative stories we also promote a *distinctive epistemology*, i.e. a way of knowing, in this case associated with an encounter with those beyond our normal network of friends and family: this experience of learning from those who are different from us opens us to the expectation that the stranger may carry an insight – rather than a threat.

Notes

1 Quoted in Daniel Taylor, *The Healing Power of Stories* (Dublin: Gill and Macmillan, 1996), p. 12. (Daniel Taylor has republished his book privately under the title '*Tell me a Story: The Life Shaping Power of our Stories*'. Copies

can be obtained from the London Mennonite Centre, email: lmc@menno.org.uk, telephone: 020 8340 8775).

2 Ibid., p. 11.

3 This story took place long before shopkeepers had the injunction not to sell cigarettes to children.

4 Ibid., p. 17.

5 Sally Trench in her book *Bury Me in My Boots* (London: Hodder and Stoughton Ltd, 1968) recalls how her mother encouraged her to always keep sixpence in her pocket so that she could have it available to give to a homeless person. Sally Trench went on to found a network of provision for homeless people at a time when such needs where scarcely acknowledged by mainstream agencies.

6 Taylor, op. cit., p. 15.

7 That is not to say that the person must be alone, in fact often the person will be part of a group. The idea of generative stories being person specific is to distinguish generative stories from stories in the media or in literature – all of which have the capacity to shape our future decisions and attitudes.

8 M. Minkler and K. M. Roe *Grandmothers as Care Givers – Children of the Crack Cocaine Epidemic* (New York: Sage, 1983).

9 Klaus Riegel 'The Dialectics of Human Development' in *American Psychologist* 31: 689.

10 My hunch is that the distinction between formal and dialectical logic may be the basis of the generational difference in attitude to certain choruses and modern hymns. It is not so much the tune or rhythm that dismays, but the expression of right-answer or formal logic. In contrast, traditional hymns tend to be respectful of dialectical logic. More controversial still is the possibility that our way of relating to the Bible may be very much informed by our preference for formal or dialogical logic.

11 Taylor, op. cit, p. 11.

12 Martha Nussbaum, 'Narrative emotions: Beckett's genealogy of love', *Ethics* 98: 225-54.

13 Taylor, op. cit, p. 18.
14 Peter Laslett, *A Fresh Map of Life* (London: Weidenfield and Nicholson, 1989).
15 The latest development of the new map of life is the eschewing of generativity. The number of women declining to have children has emerged even more suddenly than the increased longevity of the vast majority of the population. The implications of this are huge and rarely alluded to because it requires a challenge to some of the implicit almost 'holy' values of the dominant culture.
16 Ibid., p. 55.
17 This sidestepping of 'messy particulars' and focus on 'universal principles' is why the application of rationalism to more and more aspects of life creates an 'iron cage'. See chapter 2.
18 Ibid., p. 55.
19 Romans 14.
20 Charles Elliott, *Memory and Salvation* (London: Darton, Longman and Todd, 1995), p. 11.
21 Ross Parker, *Healing Wounded History* (London: Darton, Longman and Todd, 2001), pp. 44 and 40.
22 Taylor, op. cit, p. 85.
23 Walter Brueggermann, *Always in the Shadow of Empire* in Michael L. Budde and Robert W. Brimlow (eds), *The Church as Counterculture* (New York: State University Press, 2000), p. 52.
24 Ibid., p. 85.
25 In the Macpherson Report, institutional racism is defined as 'The collective failure of an organization to provide appropriate and professional service to people because of their colour, culture or ethnic origin.' Institutional racism consists of 'Processes, attitudes and behaviour that amount to discrimination through unwitting prejudice, ignorance, thoughtlessness and racist stereotyping.'
26 Ibid., p. 19.
27 This is a further example of the principle of obliquity. A

project to befriend frail, elderly people might not have been nearly as successful in meeting its objective as this bank holiday scheme to provide meals proved to be in relation to generating genuine friendship as well as bridging social capital.

5

The Suburban Challenge

The definition of *suburban* makes me wince: 'Having characteristics that are regarded as belonging especially to life in the suburbs of a city; having the inferior manners, the narrowness of view, etc. attributed to residents in the suburbs'.[1] I live in Croydon which is about as suburban as it gets. This unflattering characterization of suburban living as the place of narrowness of view is because those who live there are assumed to have a story-thin existence. Regularity, predictability and decency are likely to be the norm, along with comfort and security and one anticipates being spared the disruptions and offensiveness that are associated with deeply urban settings. Such undisturbed convenience, reliability and comfort may be the world's prescription for a satisfied life, however, from a Gospel perspective, living a life that is devoid of struggle and hope is a bad thing.

This is not to suggest that struggle is not present in suburban contexts. It most certainly is. However, the pressures are such that inadequacies and woes are kept in the closet, under wraps, out of the neighbours' view. This pressure for privacy, and even pretence, carries a double jeopardy. Intuitively we know that pretence and denial are unhealthy states but it also means that support is forgone. Furthermore, pretence, and the associated dishonesty, can make people hard to be loved and cherished. One of the biggest challenges to those who minister in suburban and well-heeled communities is to be moved to compassion and agape when those to whom one ministers are practised in denying or disguising their vulnerability.

The pressure for privacy combined with regularity and predictability of life means that the messages that dominate are likely to reinforce the mainstream view that competitiveness, pursuit of self-interest, a degree of competence and keeping out of trouble, provide the essential ingredients for a happy and successful life. However, evidence is accumulating that this recipe, which brings unprecedented scope for indulgence and style, may be a cul-de-sac. Research shows that access to more and more luxury does not translate into satisfaction with life. Study after study now show that after households have achieved sufficient income to meet their basic needs, their 'happiness' level is virtually unaffected by subsequent increases in income. Yet despite the consistency of this finding throughout the Western world, when psychologists ask us what change in our circumstances would bring the biggest improvement to our lives, the most frequent response is likely to be 'more money'.[2] In short, our income, once it reaches a level above subsistence, does not significantly influence the level of our well-being. There are other, less tangible factors that have an impact on well-being compared with affluence,[3] although our actions suggest that this is another area of denial that plagues suburban living.

Here is the rub. The Church, like every other agency, finds it hard to challenge the dishonesty and denial that infect suburban and affluent living. Challenging 'the mainstream' risks biting the hand that feeds us, and risks onlookers inspecting our lifestyle and wagging their heads as they find it no different from their own. Talk is cheaper than authentic action in relation to the afflictions of suburban life. So far the Church has found it is more acceptable to speak up on behalf of the poor than to confront the mainstream culture which forms us so extensively. Furthermore, the terrain of urban and liberation theology is more the stuff of drama and passion; in comparison, suburban theology sounds a little sad. Theology derived from Hyacinth Bouquet in 'Keeping Up Appearances' is hardly the most inspiring prospect, and more than this, it might also be a little too close for comfort for most readers and for the author. For I, like so many others, use my affluence, modest as it might be, to buy security and pleasure. As if in a play-pen I protect myself from the raw and abrasive aspects of life. For me, like so many others, it has become:

- an affront to be cold;
- unbelievably irksome to have to get up from the couch to change TV channels;
- a habit to take foreign holidays supported by tour companies and couriers;
- a habit to use the car to travel, which not only protects from inclement weather and the exhaustion of travel, but also spares us from the demands of having to rub shoulders with strangers;
- reassuring to have the availability of 'over the counter' medication to chase away pains and discomfort.

The list of ways in which we stubbornly repress any recognition of our vulnerability and creatureliness is long and very personal. The implications of such a lifestyle are huge, with powerful, but rarely acknowledged, repercussions for our spirituality and our mental health.

'The Cross' taken out of life

My suburban household, like most others, makes concerted efforts to avoid the raw and abrasive aspects of life. Michael Ignatieff describes the route that he takes to avoid making fraternal relations with his neighbours. In his book *The Needs of Strangers*,[4] Ignatieff begins with a description of those who shop at the weekly market held in the North London street where he lives. He focuses on the elderly people who pick over the second-hand clothes on the various stalls. Not only does he perceive their poverty, but he also perceives their isolation. Their children are likely to have moved to the suburbs or further afield, and their new neighbours only stay for short periods before resettling somewhere else.

In the local post office Ignatieff and the pensioners find themselves in the same queue, and it is here where he sees a parable of modern relationships between strangers. He writes, 'Their needs and their entitlements establish a silent relationship between us.' He reflects that although they remain strangers, in drawing their pension some tiny proportion of his wealth is transferred to them. He goes on to observe that 'They are dependent on the state, not upon me, and we are both glad of it.'

Through the mechanism of the state, and its million tiny capillaries, we are able to boast that we are indeed our neighbour's keeper – even though our neighbour remains a stranger. And in this way, we who inhabit the suburbs have contrived to be the Samaritan, who attends to the needs of the stranger, *as well as* priest and Levite, who both walk on by, spurning both encounter and involvement. It is an extraordinary human invention that those to whom we in the suburbs give help remain strangers to us. However, this contrivance carries a hidden cost. The absence of such face-to-face encounters lessens the likelihood of having a life healthily populated by generative stories that open our eyes to the possibility of fraternal relations with strangers.

When we journey out with the anticipation that the stranger is as our brother or sister, we both increase the likelihood of having a story-rich life, and open ourselves to the likelihood of transformation. However, this requires us to rise above the fear of being overwhelmed by the potential demands of the stranger, and the disruption that could be brought upon our well-ordered lives. Community ministry and other structures of participation that a church might initiate need to coax, support and entice suburbanites to partake of such transformational encounters, but to do so *without power*. Many of my suburban neighbours, and I too, could claim that we have extensive encounters with strangers and with those who live lives that are often assaulted by raw and abrasive experiences. My neighbours are teachers, nurses, probation officers and so on. However, as providers of these public services, the balance of power and status is always in their, I mean *our*, favour.[5] The transformational potency of being without power in an encounter is essential to holistic mission. However, those of us who live in suburban settings, in most of our encounters, even with strangers, are the ones in the position of power, whether through professional standing or by virtue of having the financial status of buyers.

I am aware that nurses and doctors might already be protesting, as well as wishing that they really did have power. Much of their day-to-day experience involves being confronted by their powerlessness. It is important to acknowledge this. The possibility of being overwhelmed by anxiety and distress is a real issue that confronts those who work in our hospitals and health centres, and it is here that a combination of professional practice and institutional policies and procedures comes into play.[6] To provide protection from such continual assaults from tragedy, death and inadequacy, procedures and policies have developed, both formally and informally. Whilst no one would wish to deny clinicians such strategies and tactics to ensure self-preservation and protection, these policies and procedures often lead to the accumulation of power – despite recurring powerlessness in relation to saving life and restoring quality to people's lives.

Anxiety prompted by the fear of being overwhelmed is not limited to those who are confronted by their powerlessness as caring professionals. Anxiety[7] is an organizing principle for our lives, and particularly for suburbanites. I have my life under control ... I use Lent to kick the alcohol habit just to reassure myself that I still can ... I watch the cholesterol level ... get my teeth looked over regularly ... and try to make sure my diet has enough of a thing called roughage ... I am cautious about whom I let into my house ... I have saved for a pension. ... Yet I am anxious. I am anxious because I know that something, maybe a 36 bus, a dirty bomb or bowel cancer, will surely come and overwhelm me. Even the reassurance of eternal life, which I rejoice in, does not stop my primitive, animal response of anxiety. My hunch is that anxiety is endemic in suburbia. The more life is experienced as sorted, the greater the fear that something will come and upset the applecart.

Ernest Becker wrote a celebrated book about just this thing. He called it *The Denial of Death*. Becker was an acclaimed depth psychologist, working both as a practitioner and an academic. As a depth psychologist he was committed to the reality of the sub-conscious and unconscious as influences upon our behaviour. He was a follower of Freud, acknowledging that some awarenesses were so intense that they would probably be repressed. Like Freud, Becker had considered matters of a sexual nature to be the material most likely to be repressed and therefore generate neurosis, or even worse. However, in *The Denial of Death* Becker departs from the classic Freudian interpretation of repressed behaviour, and articulates his mounting unease at the focus of Freudian analysis. Becker suggests that the primary repression of those of us in the West is the awareness of death. He suggests that the level of narcissism that has been fostered makes it impossible to tolerate the thought of death. Added to this, the dominance of a scientific world view has reduced the perspective on our existence to that of being '*selves*', when once we were possessors of souls.[8] In such a context, Becker comments that 'Man is literally split in two: he has an awareness of his own splendid uniqueness in that he sticks out of nature with a towering majesty, and yet he goes back into the ground a few feet in order blindly and dumbly to rot and disappear forever. It is a terrifying dilemma to be in and to have to live with.'[9]

As if writing for the suburban scene, Becker, quotes Otto Rank, 'If a man is the more normal, healthy and happy, the more he can ... successfully ... repress, displace, deny, rationalize, dramatize himself and deceive others'.[10] This capacity for denial and deception is the root of the suburban dis-ease. Often in less apparently well-ordered places, people's inadequacies are so much more visible that deceit and denial are less likely to be in the ascendant. One might question whether such denial and deception actually matters, because in day-to-day functioning there is apparent effectiveness and neighbourliness and decency. However, Becker invites us to look again. He notes that 'All through history it is the normal average men who, like locusts, have laid waste to the world in order to forget themselves.'[11] This may sound extreme, however, there is justification for such an indictment. It is now recognized that the dynamic that contributed significantly to the Nazi ability to commit awful acts of cruelty on those who were once their neighbour was the dynamic of *anticipatory obedience*. When people are anxious and insecure, the most obvious way of gaining reassurance is to gain an accolade or reward, or to be thought well of, by those in positions of power and authority. I find myself wanting to do this all the time. The sure-fire way of impressing one's superior is not just by doing what is asked of you, but by *anticipating* what they want to see happen. Such skill is often called initiative, and when tuned into the implicit or explicit values of the organization it will probably be well rewarded in the annual performance review. It is an art that is well honed in suburbanites with careers in comparison to those who just 'go to work'.

Depth psychologists urge people to grow beyond this dependence that has its roots in anxiety and insecurity. Jung used the concept of *individuation* to describe that state of maturity which is marked by independence of thinking, seeing and acting, when the person is no longer constrained by the need for the protective approval of those who are powerful. Becker suggests that the heroism required to achieve this individuation is too much for most of us. He writes, 'Individuation is a very daring venture, precisely because it separates the person from comfortable beyonds. It takes a strength and courage the average man doesn't have and couldn't even understand – as Jung so well points out. The most terrifying burden of the creature is to be isolated, which is what happens in individuation: one separates himself out from the herd. This moves the person to the sense of being completely crushed and annihilated because he sticks out so much, (and) has to carry so much in himself.'[12]

Becker joins with Kierkegaard and William James in insisting that for ordinary, routine guys like you and me, the most viable route to individuation is via faith in God. These three commentators suggest that *healthy* religion provides a framework which supports, rather than suppresses, the process of individuation. The alternative to embracing a God who is bigger than death itself, is according to Becker, to fall prey to a self-consuming and destructive individualist framework of heroic living. Becker and other depth psychologists describe the journey of separating ourselves from automatic cultural actions as an act of heroism because of the courage it requires to cease to merge into the suburban world that surrounds us. However, most dwellers of suburbia are not cut out to be heroes. Nevertheless, both for the sake of the integrity of our faith and for our mental health, we need to find a way of separating ourselves out of the common pool of shared meanings. The Church has so far shirked the responsibility for enabling people to embark on the task of Godly-supported individuation, or separating ourselves out from the conventional behaviour of suburban dwellers.

Involvement in community ministry and other structures of participation helps the process of Godly-supported individuation. This is not as naive as it may first appear. A case has already been made that involvement in community ministry can contribute to a story-rich life, and that the stories that form us take us beyond superficiality of personality and make us into people with *character* or integrity. Those with story-rich lives are those who are likely to be distinguishable from the crowd. But there is more to it than just this. Becker writes, 'The defeat of despair is not mainly an intellectual problem for a person, but a problem of self-stimulation by movement. Beyond a given point man is not helped by more knowing, but only by living and doing in a partly self-forgetful way.'[13] What Becker is saying is that despair comes upon us when we become aware of our inability to be heroic, and our inability to act honourably on our perceptions and insights. The way through this despair is not by thinking harder and more intensely, but by *doing* something that helps us to forget ourselves and moves us, if only ever so slightly, in the direction of our intimation of what is true.

Journeying out via community ministry enables us to move, if only ever so slightly, in the direction of our intimation of what is true and to do so in a partly self-forgetful way. For those of us who know our inability to be heroes, it enables us to take risks within limits and with a structure of support. Community ministry and other structures of participation which help us express venturesome love could be the therapy that is needed for those of us who have been able to protect ourselves from the raw and abrasive aspects of life and the risk of being overwhelmed. Once again, to quote Becker, 'To live is to engage in experience at least partly on the terms of the experience itself. (A person) has to stick his neck out in the action without any guarantees about satisfaction or safety.'[14] The essence of community ministry is not so much that it carries a threat of danger, but it is about being party to an encounter, stripped of any power, and therefore being open to helplessness and failure in the face of the other's struggle. My brother's struggle can become my struggle because of our capacity for empathy, a gracious gift granted to us by our Heavenly Father.

This capacity for a step-by-step journey outwards involves practising 'sticking one's neck out', allowing ourselves to be separated from the herd and journeying towards our potential to be a hero – or a Child of God. I therefore repeat my point, so long as we fall prey to viewing community involvement as solely about engagement with the needs of the wider community, we miss this key pastoral potential for challenging the conventional culture of suburban living. Journeying out in a suburban setting is about far more than meeting need, for it is a radical act to invite those who are cocooned in play-pen living to strip themselves of power and rise above the anxiety associated with the risk of being overwhelmed. For those of us who escape and shroud ourselves in the Sunday supplements, community ministry can enable us to move beyond the insidious psychological despair associated with the challenge of individuation. In the context of the play-pen living that dominates suburbia journeying out via community ministry and other structures of participation is class treason.

The journey to encounter struggle

There is a huge weakness in all this, and it was expressed to me most cogently by a church member, resident in a very comfortable suburban district in north-west London. I had spent ten minutes telling of the imagination, courage and effectiveness of the structure of participation associated with the churches' winter night shelters that were being set up in inner London. With huge regret in his voice, he articulated what I am sure many others were thinking, 'If we had homeless people round here we could do that'. And there we have it: the opportunity to encounter and engage with those who struggle is a scarce resource in suburban contexts. The obvious hardship, which makes the community ministry model viable in an inner urban context, is a rare commodity in suburbia.

However, obvious hardship is not a rare commodity in our world. Community ministry does not have to focus on the local, it can also promote engagement with issues that are far away. The transformational encounter that is so essential to the potency of community ministry may require a flight from Heathrow, not so much for the sun and sea, but to come alongside those who are ensnarled in the raw and abrasive aspects of life. This makes for a very different type of package holiday to that which is typical of play-pen living.

In one of the smarter west London boroughs a local GP has a friend who lives in the Philippines. Together they have set up a micro-credit organization. The GP goes round members of his congregation to ask them to write a cheque for £100. This sum is then made available to a household in Manila who are reliant on some form of personal enterprise if they are to escape from crippling poverty. The capacity for enterprise does not seem to be in short supply, but the capital needed to launch an enterprise is scarce. It is this gap that the GP's friends and neighbours have begun to address in a very modest, but structured way. Each contributor receives a profile of the Filipino household and an outline of the venture they are trying to develop. If the household becomes able to repay the loan, that sum is 'recycled' and made available to another household.

Every two years, the London-based GP invites three or four of the west London sponsors to visit Manila with him to see things at firsthand, and to meet the network of households that are linked through the micro-credit scheme.

This modest micro-credit scheme most obviously promotes positive change by providing otherwise non-existent investment capital to those in chronic poverty. However the significance of this modest venture rests not so much in its overt intention, but in harnessing the principle of obliquity, i.e. by inviting people to visit Manila, it sets in train a host of other graceful dynamics:

♦ it enables modestly respectable people to stick their necks out and begin to separate themselves from the crowd;
♦ it provides a structure which enables those who have life 'sorted' to embrace the possibility of being overwhelmed;
♦ the encounter with those who know deeply about struggle creates a 'thin place' where only a tissue separates us from an awareness of God and transformation.

To illustrate this cascade of grace I sketch a possible scenario:

Jim and Sue are invited to a supper party hosted by the neighbours up the road. It's a leaving party as the host and hostess are soon to retire and move to Devon. The conversation during the evening naturally focuses on the freedom that comes with retirement and the scope for leisure and hobbies. Those still at work can only speak of holidays that are being planned, but in the midst of such suburban conversations, the story that Jim and Sue carry enables them to stand out from the crowd and show themselves as people willing to stick their neck out.

Someone says that they are thinking of booking a fortnight in Cuba, another comments on the nature of the Castro regime and yet another talks of the frequent business trips to increasingly entrepreneurial Poland. At this point Sue says that she and Jim are going to Manila next month to visit some of the people in the shanty townships, because they are part of a micro-credit project run by a GP who goes to their church....

The story that Sue and Jim have to hand, even before they visit Manila, let alone after, enables them to define themselves as different from their neighbours and as people with different values from the mainstream. However, their story may also be attractive to others. Quietly people will ponder whether they too could be party to experiences that are a rich source of genuine stories that go deep and speak of abiding and humane values. They too might like to have a story-rich life like Sue and Jim seem to have discovered, for in telling the story they are party to, others might also glimpse their 'potential selves'. Furthermore, Jim and Sue's story may be more attractive to their suburban neighbours than at any other time in modern history.

The experience economy

In their epoch-making book, *The Experience Economy*, Pine and Gilmore write, 'This is new: experiences represent an existing but previously unarticulated *genre of economic output*'.[15] The newness that they refer to is the shift from the marketing and promotion of commodities to the new business of marketing experiences. What has happened is that those of us who dwell in suburbia may well have had our fill of commodities. After all, there are only so many times that one can have the kitchen refitted, fill the wardrobes to bust and shop at Ikea, without cluttering the house so much that the Swedish idyll of clear surfaces and elegant lines becomes a mockery. Our suburban households are full and only the 'Friends' generation and younger retain an appetite to shop till they drop. But even they are not immune to the attraction of *experiences*. The spawning of coffee shop after coffee shop illustrates our new willingness to partake of, or should I say pay for, an experience, and not just a commodity.

Pine and Gilmore, writing for the business community, are alert to the limitations of competing on price, highlighting how this approach ultimately undermines growth and profitability. As an alternative, they urge businesses to embrace the experience option. *Experience* has always been at the heart of the entertainment and leisure industries but Pine and Gilmore urge businesses to devise or stage experiences in a way that *engages* people and doesn't just entertain them.[16] In the emerging experience economy the more a business can create an experience that engages people in a personal and memorable way the more that business will be successful.

This new emphasis has a number of implications for those of us concerned with encouraging people to hear and respond to the Gospel. Pine and Gilmore describe success in the experience economy coming about by engaging people in a personal and memorable way. Most churches would feel that this is *their* very intention. Furthermore, with the advent of the experience economy, we can be confident that an invitation to participate in events that promote generative stories will be well received. The shift from preoccupation with consumer goods to engaging experiences really does make church-going an activity whose time has come. Pine and Gilmore recommend that businesses promote engaging and personalized experiences and here once again churches are well placed. For example, there is no better approach to engaging people in a personal and memorable way than via spiritual direction, one of the classic resources of the Church through the role of priest or pastor.

Spiritual direction essentially involves people reflecting on their experiences, and exploring how their experiences help or inhibit them in their relationship with God. The importance of reflecting on experience was considered in the previous chapter. The case was made that failure to reflect on experiences could feed stereotyping, and the absence of reflection in relation to the emerging experience economy is a worry. Goethe observes that human flourishing requires that we must plunge into experience *and* then reflect on the meaning of it. Both are necessary because, as he goes on to comment, all reflecting and no plunging drives us mad; all plunging and no reflecting and we are brutes.[17] Those of us who dwell in suburbia are the likely targets of those who wish to restore their profitability by coaxing us to plunge into experience and we need to heed Goethe's warning that this can make us brutes.

There are other concerns that we should have in relation to the growing experience economy. 'Late capitalism' invites collusion between affluent communities that benefit from high returns from the market economy. This means that the experiences that will be marketed will pander not only to our brutal nature but also our vulnerability to the narcotic effect of trivial and potentially addictive experiences. My concern is rooted in Otto Rank's observation that when the self is overvalued, we cannot risk our self-image being challenged and shown wanting, either to others or to ourselves.[18] In a culture that encourages the huge valuing of self, the experiences we allow ourselves to encounter cannot afford to threaten the magical, impervious confection that is involved in the public presentation of self. We are a generation that cannot face too much reality entering our lives. So the experience we opt for will be of the Rainforest Café rather than the rainforest. The beautiful island of Jamaica will be sampled from the safety of the holiday village, sweat will appear on our brows as a result of the exercise bicycle and rumour has it that we are too posh to push when it comes to childbirth.

Kierkegaard did not need to live in our time to understand these things. He already saw them prefigured in his own day because of his acute capacity to perceive the dishonesty that abounds in the way in which we, throughout human history, have engaged with each other and with life itself. Kierkegaard recognized the cost of such dishonesty, and the games we play in order to fool others and ourselves. He wrote lucidly and extensively about the anxiety that is provoked by our inability to face up to both our vulnerability as well as our potential. In exposing this terrifying fragility at the heart of the human enterprise Kierkegaard has provided a rich seam of analysis, relevant to both theology and depth psychology. One particular concept that he developed is particularly relevant to suburban souls, especially when confronted by the experience economy: *Philistine behaviour.*

Car advertising has been quick to enter the experience business. Adverts have shifted from emphasizing a car's performance to emphasizing the distinctive experience that the car can bring about. Perhaps the most explicit example is produced by Honda. Quietly presented above the image of one of Honda's gleaming new models is the wisdom of Soichiro Honda: 'Life is measured by the number of times your soul is deeply stirred'.[19] This example of the profound being used in the service of the inconsequential is an example of Kierkegaard's concern about Philistine behaviour. He writes, 'Devoid of imagination, as the Philistine always is, he lives in a certain trivial province of experience as to how things go, what is possible, what usually occurs ... Philistinism tranquillizes itself in the trivial.'[20] Our capacity for being engrossed in and by trivial behaviour is extraordinary. When this is combined with our rarely acknowledged propensity for addictive behaviour, the advent of the experience economy may entrap and bewitch suburbanites as much if not more than consuming goods and services.

It could be concluded that suburbanites like me are a pretty worthless, self-deceiving, other-deceiving, wimpish and feeble life form, unworthy of sympathy or liberation. Except that Kierkegaard understands what has befallen those of us who live secure lives, and he sympathizes with our plight. He questions why we accept such a life dominated by trivia. He surmises that it is because we are fearful of the full horizon of experience, and that this fear is the norm. It is according to Kierkegaard, and subsequent analysts, a *normal neurosis*. Most of us figure out how to live our lives safely within a given set of social rules, ensuring that our lives are maintained at a low level of intensity, avoiding being knocked off balance by threatening or challenging experiences. It is not about being blameworthy in relation to such a plight. It is about being vulnerable, paradoxically creative and yet helpless creatures, with an intimation that we are special.

The Church in coaxing and enticing people to journey out must heed the fearfulness with which sticking one's neck out is surrounded. In the context of the angst that is generated by unlimited horizons, the legitimacy and importance of enticement need to be taken into account. Community ministry provides an amenable gradient as well as the promise of an enticing, story-rich life. Involvement in a structure of participation associated with community ministry permits encounters to take place within bounds that give reassurance that one can risk being overwhelmed even though in this encounter we will be without power.

The step-by-step gradualness of sticking one's neck out via involvement in community ministry protects and spares the suburban dweller from becoming defensive in response to a fearsome challenge, and it safeguards against inappropriate and naive heroism. Whilst the therapeutic and even transformational potential of the encounters generated by community ministry cannot be guaranteed, such encounters will, for sure, produce material which warrants reflection. When the process of reflecting is put alongside the encounter with those who know deeply about struggle, and with situations where the threat of being overwhelmed remains significant, then we increase our openness to a cascade of grace:

Our hearts will be moistened

This phrase used by John Donne grows out of the awareness that preoccupation with self-interest hardens our heart. Through the grace of God those of us seduced by play-pen existence can, 'by proxy', partake of struggle and the raw and abrasive aspects of life, and this awakens our imagination. Compassion begins to flow as we begin to see 'the person' behind the hardship. Though we ourselves may have suffered very little, it is in the nature and power of encounter and story that for a few moments, it is possible for someone else's suffering to become our suffering. The root meaning of compassion is 'to suffer with' and it is this process that enables me to shed my suburban defendedness and sample the smack of vulnerability in an open and attentive manner.

The dignity and stamina of the human spirit may be glimpsed

The encounter with the person who experiences the raw and abrasive aspects of life and hearing his or her underlying story exposes the choices they have had to make in their lives. The choices we make reveal the values we live by and speak of our character. Those beset by the harshness of life can communicate an unfettered humility and endurance. Such capacities seem dated in a suburban world, but secretly each of us intuits that such resilience is worth more than it is credited with. Those who have faced repeatedly the risk of being overwhelmed can expose the sham confidence and self-regard that lurks within suburban hearts. Dignified behaviour takes on a different hue when it is expressed by the lowliest people.

The all-encompassing and subtle nature of sin begins to be recognized

The encounter with the person who struggles to maintain a family in the shanty towns of Manila, or to eke a living from the parched land of Eritrea allows the story that underpins their circumstances to be heard and understood. This can lead to a sense within the hearer of 'there but for the grace of God go I', and this is an important step in recognizing that blaming others for the circumstances in which they find themselves is a senseless approach. Hearing the underlying story of the person enables the nature of our human *plight* to be recognized and once we allow ourselves to be frank about the vulnerability of the human condition there is scope for a more informed and mature understanding of the nature of sin. When we journey out without power as a shield and protector all we can offer is a willingness to listen and a commitment to try to understand. Thus being stripped of power enables the underlying stories to be encountered, and such encounters will probably make us more tolerant and forgiving of moral failure and at the same time they will convince us of the reality and necessity of the moral dimension of life.

Furthermore, we begin to recognize both perceptible and imperceptible ways in which each one of us contributes to a predicament that defies human will and agency. Sin ceases to be just about personal morality and becomes something far more potent, a force that mires and infects even our best intentions. We begin to see how all of us are caught up in sin, even those of us who dwell securely and decently in suburbia.

The inclination of institutions to organize things for the convenience and benefit of those on the inside begins to be recognized

An encounter with those who face hardship (or an encounter with their story) enables the messy particulars of their circumstances to be unfurled, and as a result the limited response of bureaucratic, 'legal-rational' organizations is revealed. Although established with the aim of helping those in hardship, their very 'rationality' based on universal principals and theories works against drawing alongside the situations that overwhelm people. And it becomes apparent that public bodies and other agencies tend to sidestep so many messy particulars. Inevitably, over time, agencies established to work on behalf of those in need develop so many conditions and boundaries that the help they offer becomes restricted and conditional. However, like so much else in life, this dynamic has to be seen to be believed. But this is not all. The boundaries that are maintained lead to benefits to the professional class that administers the agency. The task of supervising to ensure the correct application of rules and regulations counts for more than the task of tending those in need. The meaningful careers of those who dwell in suburbia are laid open and prove less commendable than we had surmised. This conclusion is not rooted in cynicism but in the recognition of the extensiveness and inescapable nature of structural sin.

The achievement of 'deep literacy'

Deep literacy is the name Paulo Freire gives to the ability to *read* how power is exercised and distributed.[21] It requires us to acknowledge that our perceptions are not open and innocent but shaped by myriad sources, and are shaped in a way which maintains the *status quo*. There are patterns that underpin our apparent common sense and these patterns repeatedly favour some and disadvantage others. Our suburban investment in common sense gets challenged, as serving a sectional interest rather than everyone's interests, and certainly not serving the interests of the poorest and most vulnerable. Deep literacy requires the willingness to question what we think we know, and this willingness brings with it scope for dialogue with those who see and experience the world differently from us. The encounter with those who are excluded helps us to see the power of unexamined assumptions. Thus an encounter with those who are excluded is a source of epistemological insight into what is otherwise hidden from us.

Recognition that all dwell in a continual state of vulnerability

Exposure to the vulnerability of those who have no money to routinely protect themselves from the raw and abrasive aspects of life can enable the more affluent to acknowledge our own vulnerability. There is an invitation at the heart of every story that is shared. It is the invitation 'You come too'. In this invitation resides the formative and potentially healing power of an encounter with those who cannot deny or disguise their vulnerability. The veneer of security that money can give is exposed as insubstantial in the face of the inevitability of sickness and death. In the absence of open acknowledgement of our vulnerability we live with a constant apprehension about what *might* happen. In owning and accepting vulnerability as a non-negotiable fact of life the route to honest thinking and acting opens up before us.

These realizations are important staging points on the journey towards Godly supported individuation. They are a consequence of reflecting on an encounter with those who are vulnerable or excluded. They prepare those of us who enjoy the suburbs to stick our neck out and speak of a different reality. No longer are we as prone to the delusion that most things are right with the world – and our world in particular. Community ministry, when it travels to the suburbs, has as its aim the transformation of suburbia. Community ministry can model a committed lifestyle sufficiently attractive to entice people away from the addictive lifestyle of play-pen existence and do this without provoking dysfunctional defensiveness and guilt within those of us for whom such play-pen living is the norm.

Notes

1 *The Shorter Oxford English Dictionary/Britannica World Language Dictionary* (Oxford: Clarendon Press).

2 See the work of Diener, Sandvik, Seidlitz and Diener in 'The Relationship Between Income and Subjective Well-Being: Relative or Absolute?' in *Social Indicators Research* 28: 195–223.

3 The Cabinet Office Report (2003) 'Life Satisfaction Study' comments: 'Religion drive[s] up life satisfaction. It has been estimated that in the US ... bi-weekly church attendance [has] the happiness equivalent of a doubling of money income'. p. 3.

4 Michael Ignatieff, *The Needs of Strangers* (London: Hogarth Press, 1984), p. 10.

5 There is a straightforward way of exposing where power lies. It involves a threefold question: Who decides? Who wins? Who loses? There will always be some who decide, some who win and some who lose, this is a non-negotiable feature of everyday life because power, like the air we breathe, is part and parcel of life. However, we need to be alert to situations where repeatedly the same people or groups decide, the same people or groups win and the same people or groups lose. In these instances we need to exercise the hermeneutic of suspicion, i.e. begin to smell a rat!

6 See Isabel Menzies Lyth, *Containing Anxieties in Institutions* (London: Free Association Books, 1988).

7 The theme of anxiety and ways of handling anxiety will be considered in chapter 9.

8 The idea of having a soul that survives death is a 'folk' concept rather than a Christian one. For the Christian we acknowledge that we have a soul, but eternal life is a gift from God made manifest by Jesus.

9 Ernest Becker, *The Denial of Death* (New York: The Free Press, 1974), p. 26.

10 Otto Rank, *Will Therapy and Truth and Reality* (New

York: Knopf, 1936, single-volume edition 1945), p. 251.

11 Becker, op. cit., p. 187.
12 Ibid., p. 171.
13 Ibid., p. 199.
14 Ibid., p. 183.
15 B. Joseph Pine and James H Gilmore, *The Experience Economy* (Boston, Mass.: Harvard Business School Press, 1999), p. ix (italics in original).
16 Ibid., p. 30.
17 I am unable to trace from where I have obtained this reference to Goethe, but I consider it too important an observation to exclude because of this failure of mine.
18 Otto Rank, *Will Therapy and Truth and Reality* (New York: Knopf, 1936; single-volume edition, 1945), p. 151.
19 Honda's current mission statement is 'Honda: the power of dreams'.
20 Soren Kierkegaard, (1849) *The Sickness Unto Death* (Anchor Edition 1954), pp. 174–5.
21 Deep literacy or the *conscientization of people to specific cases of injustice* is a theme that runs throughout Paulo Freire's work. See Paulo Freire, *Pedagogy of the Oppressed* (London: Penguin Books, 1972).

6

Without Power

Pontius Pilate has one of the great walk on, walk off roles in the Bible. The sentences he voices are few: announcing that he can find no fault in the self proclaimed King of the Jews, offering to trade Jesus for Barabbas and ultimately washing his hands of the whole affair. However, one phrase that he utters easily gets lost in the drama of it all. In response to Jesus' comment that He came into this world to testify to the truth, Pilate replies with the cynicism befitting his role, 'What is truth?'[1]

Such realism about the slippery nature of truth was no doubt a product of Pilate's journey to power as a representative of the Roman Emperor. He would have travelled widely and have been confronted by the diversity of religions, philosophies and ways of making sense of the world. In this, Pontius Pilate bears an extraordinary resemblance to third-millennium Europeans, likewise confronted by diversity, equally bemused as to what is truth and equally unimpressed when someone claims to have particular access to the truth. The question 'What is truth?' is likely now to be found on the lips of many, and is no doubt spoken with an equally cynical tone to that of Pilate.

There is an uneasy relationship within the Christian community about 'truth'. For some Christians there is a duty to counter question, continually enquire and practise an inner duty of critique. For others truth is hermetically sealed, and therefore uncertainty and questioning are unwelcome and indicative of limp commitment. My challenge to those who believe that it is possible to embrace truth with confidence and assurance is that they may underestimate the potency and extensiveness of sin. The necessity to search for truth is a product not just of my personal sin but also a product of structural and original sin.

It has taken the sociologists and the psychologists to expose this, whilst so many theologians have worked on, oblivious to the great *journey towards truth* that we have to embrace. Furthermore, many who define themselves as out-siders or non-believers may do so because they cannot identify with, or be part of, a group of people who naively claim to have 'the truth'. It is ironic therefore that those Christians who are often most keen to share their beliefs with others, and actively proselytize, may well prompt the aliena-tion of so many who might otherwise be willing to explore faith but find assertions about the truth about God an insur-mountable hurdle.

In a post-modern context, the naivety of our approach to truth and the denial of the illusiveness of truth may be a major turn off for many who would otherwise wish to do business with God. However, it is not for the sake of being cool and up to the minute that I urge upon us a more unassuming approach to truth. It is because I take my sinfulness and that of others seriously. I am too puny and easily influenced to be confident that truth about God is safe in my hands. Further-more, I had a very humbling encounter at a stage in my life when I considered the truth about God to be straightforward.

Years ago I earned my living as a researcher for the Reli-gious Experience Research Unit. The job involved interviewing hundreds of people about whether they 'had ever been aware of or influenced by a presence or power whether they called it God or not'. One experience stands out in my mind because it forced me to acknowledge the legit-imacy and significance of 'What is truth?' in one's questing for

God. I interviewed a chap already in his seventies. He replied positively to the question designed to elicit reports of religious experience. I asked him to tell me about the time that was most important to him. He retold a wartime experience.

> He and his detachment had come under heavy fire. He began running with his fellow soldiers to take shelter in the new dugout they had just completed. But as he was running, he felt a powerful urge to run to the old dugout instead. He did so, only to see a shell land directly on the new dugout. He was the only one to survive the attack. I asked him how he made sense of the experience and he said 'My family was praying for me and I link it with that – but it's still a mystery to me.'

I came away from that interview chastened. In order to rejoice in the certainty of God's involvement in his life this chap would have had to discount the lives of five of his mates. How could it be that God would single him out for survival whilst the families of his comrades were to receive a letter of deepest regret and commiseration from the major? In the interview he confessed that for over 40 years the experience that saved his life remained a mystery to him, because he was not prepared to embrace a God who seemed to have favourites.[2] The impact of this interview on me was profound. His struggle for the truth seemed to have more integrity than my package of right answers and right beliefs. The question I was left pondering was what sort of God would reject this chap's struggle to make sense of the *truth* of God?

To take seriously that we all have to struggle for truth does not mean that we are working completely in the dark. There have been revelations and, God willing, there will continue to be revelations which can inform our seeing and understanding. But in our earthbound existence we must take seriously that we cannot, with confidence, embrace truth. We may glimpse truth, we may sense truth, but we can never possess it. We can only hope to journey towards it. The Gospel, as God's distinctive revelation, is full of truth.

119

However, our ability, as sinful, malleable people, to make sense of its insights and incorporate such revelation into our lives is inadequate. Pilate in uttering 'What is truth?' issues an important warning that truth is something humankind must continually struggle for and may glimpse but never reliably hold.

There are two huge implications from this. The first is that we must be humble or sit lightly to what we think we know as truth. The second implication is more challenging still. Given the pervasiveness of sin on our earth and in our lives our understanding of the Gospel will be *partisan*. This means our seeing and understanding is not just partial but skewed. Furthermore, the skew is not random, for what we take as truth is invariably shaped or biased by vested interest. This is strong meat and needs some justification.

The sin at the level of our perceiving

Sociology demolishes our innocence in relation to truth because it exposes the subtle, and not so subtle, dynamics of vested interest and the power that enables some people's interests to dominate, or even triumph, over others. Sociologists, well aware that they risk getting lost in a sea of relativism, urge us to take seriously the fact that our seeing and knowing are all contaminated by a dominant culture which serves the interests of the most powerful in society. They use the term *hegemony* to describe this dynamic that runs through all aspects of our social existence and shapes our seeing and understanding in ways that reinforce and serve established power relations. Raymond Williams comments that hegemony 'saturates society'.[3] Hegemony creates a *common sense* framework, legitimated by the media, and it is reinforced by routine practices and assumptions. The saturation is so all encompassing that it becomes impossible to envisage any alternatives. Hegemony engineers consensus about the way things are, limits our perception and inhibits questioning. The power of hegemony is such that life is assumed to take the shape and rhythm that it does to the extent that it is taken as natural and therefore beyond question.

This sociological observation may appear extreme in its cynicism. However it is an insight which must be treated with respect by those who would claim to be committed to a journey towards truth and the Kingdom of God. For the power and subtlety of the hegemonic, or taken-for-granted, order of things can lead us into trespass. A potent example of this capacity to engender unquestionable attitudes and understanding comes from my first job in the Church:

My first employer in the Church was a Council for Social Responsibility. Just five years before I began working for this department it had operated under the name of 'Moral Welfare', and before that it was called 'Rescue and Preventative Work'.

The origin of this work, 100 years before, was to rescue the young women who drifted into town from the countryside and who, in their desperation to gain food and shelter, might resort to prostitution. So the Church set up training schools to prepare these women to go 'into service' in local 'well-to-do' households or train to work in the new factories that needed more and more workers. Within ten years of establishing these projects a new issue emerged – the task of responding to those women, who despite being rescued, trained and placed in service, became pregnant. So, alongside the training schools, homes were set up where the woman (or girl) could give birth and from where her child would be adopted. As soon as she was free of her baby, the woman would return to the household where she was in service. However, if while 'in service' the woman became pregnant again then she risked being categorized as morally defective. To become pregnant a second time served as proof of her immorality.

In the filing cabinet in my office were the old volumes, full of casenotes, relating to these immoral women. The organization was not only lawfully empowered to label women, but to then condemn them to a hospital for the morally defective for the rest of their lives.[4]

The seductive and physical power of the 'gentleman' in the household in which the woman was employed as a servant would never have been considered or even 'seen'. Not least, because the very definition of 'gentleman' precluded the possibility of him forcing his attention on a young woman. The credence given to Eve as the route by which sin entered the world would have added to the common sense view that a young woman from the lower classes would be prone to moral defectiveness.

Those writing the case notes took their task very seriously, but it is unlikely they would have perceived the outworking of hegemony in relation to what they were doing. Or, if they did, it would be unlikely that they would have had the courage to speak out against the practice that they implemented.

Thus, the power of the hegemonic ordering affects our seeing and understanding in such a way as to protect the powerful and victimize the weak, and this applies today as much as it did 100 years ago. For those who ran the organization and imposed the label and a lifetime's hospitalization on the women the unfairness of their actions would have remained imperceptible. The category 'morally defective' may have disappeared from usage today, but for much of the last 150 years, the hegemonic order, which was deeply influenced by religious authorities, made such labelling and treatment both plausible and legitimate.

That tragic labelling, written in the most elegant copper-plate handwriting in those case notes, is part of my inheritance as a woman working in the social responsibility field within the Church of England. As I sat in my office, reading those case notes, I was aware that if I had been born 60 years earlier I might have been the superintendent of the Mother and Baby Home, and I too would have written those same casenotes. I too would have been unable to see how the powerless were being victimized and the powerful remained unaccountable. I am very aware that, armed with similar power and authority, I would have seen it as my duty to condemn the women likewise.

Today, to label someone as morally defective would be outrageous: however, whilst this particular category may have lost its social power others no doubt have taken its place. The difficulty is that it is almost impossible to identify this contamination or corruption of our seeing, thinking and acting. The nature of the prevailing hegemonic order is that any attempt to unmask an oppressive force risks serious, social censure. The understandable response is to baulk at the possibility of sticking one's neck out and to opt for silence. The least painful option is likely to prevail and we take confidence in the assumption that the experts know best, just as 60 years ago the experts in moral welfare were assumed to know best. It is this insidious cowardice, absence of perspicacity and deep-seated denial which engenders sinful systems. Whilst ever we, both personally and corporately, have supped with, and courted, the powerful we risk promoting injustice and we risk mistaking the truths of the Gospel.

This business of hegemony is about our proneness to sin. No one can escape the influence of the wider, social environment. The ease with which we accommodate the powerful, and are seduced into believing and investing in common sense and switching off our critical capacity is the foundation of structural sin. None of us can be confident that we can see and understand justly and fairly, for the hegemonic smog that surrounds us confuses us and disguises things which we would otherwise refuse to tolerate. And it is those in positions of power who are most prone to the pollution associated with this engendered consensus. So it is with some relief, that 60 years on, the Church has lost its power to shore up, and even to shape, the hegemony of moral respectability.

The loyalty of the poor to the teachings of the Church, despite the Church investing so much effort in justifying the rights of their lords and masters over them, is well documented. In fact, the exceptional competence of the Church of England in maintaining social order throughout the land needs to be acknowledged. Home Secretaries today must sometimes lament the passing of the religious hegemony that prevailed for so long. For there is no more reliable and cost-effective way of maintaining law and order than by shaping people's understanding, to the extent that they internalize what is acceptable behaviour and willingly police each other. It would be wrong to think that this state of affairs was forcibly imposed upon a resistant peasantry (although there were occasions when this was so). Hegemony is far subtler than this. For it carries security and reassurance. Very few of us can resist the temptation of being part of the popular or dominant culture,[5] even when we might occupy a disadvantageous or oppressed position.

The Church has now almost granted Karl Marx the status of prophet (this in itself is a major hegemonic shift), and it means we can learn from his insights rather than resist them. In particular we should heed his idea of *false consciousness*. False consciousness refers to our capacity to be beguiled. False consciousness describes the capacity of religion, and other ideological systems, to captivate people even when it does not serve their interests. Religions, and that includes Christianity, can become putty in the hands of the powerful. Powerful regimes, supported by compliant, and usually substantially rewarded, religious authorities, can generate a view of God that serves the interests of their regime. False consciousness is an insidious and potent dynamic that can captivate us all, to the extent that we do not know what we do. However, there is good news, for there is a way through this mire of unbeknown sinfulness. In order to express an alternative perception of the truth to that which prevails[6] we have to separate ourselves from that internalized lust for power that has driven us since our lost innocence in the Garden of Eden.

Sluggish theology

It is extraordinary that theologians did not identify the concept of hegemony before sociologists. Not only is hegemony the main dynamic that contributes to structural sin, it also puts the spotlight on the reality of original sin: for hegemony is about letting somebody – or some snake – tell us what to think and what to do. Mainstream theology has been strangely silent and reluctant to draw attention to this fact of our social existence. There is a far from edifying explanation for this oversight. It is a sign of how ensnared the theological and ecclesiastical realms have been to the hegemonic order. This should not cause surprise or even offence, for it is part of our plight. Those who are coopted by a power elite can scarcely avoid disseminating insights and perceptions that shore up the *status quo* and their own position of power.

Mary, Jesus' mother, in annunciating the words of the Magnificat[7] provides one of the world's most potent exposures of hegemonic order. She stuck her neck out, and saw a different order, and a *different* God from that of the mainstream, religious authorities. For she recognized that God had looked upon her, his lowly servant, with favour, and He would scatter the proud in their conceit, He would cast the mighty from their thrones, and He would fill the hungry with good things, whilst the rich would be sent away empty. The Magnificat, in all its radicalness, has been part of the traditional liturgy of the Church of England, perhaps serving as encouragement to the poor and reminding the king that he ruled solely by permission of God. Whilst ever the Church counted herself as a power and force in the land Scripture would be harnessed to support this purpose.

As well as rejoicing in the Magnificat, the Church and theologians of the past could have looked at almost any encounter that Jesus had with the Pharisees to see a challenge to the religious hegemony. The Pharisees were more than a little distressed when Jesus repeatedly taught that there were other ways of seeing and understanding life apart from the

Law which they upheld. At each point of encounter, we see Jesus challenging the world view promulgated by those who benefited most from the *status quo*, culminating in his journey to Jerusalem, the centre of power in the land. And as happens so often to those who persist in challenging otherwise unquestioned assumptions, rather than allow Jesus' perspectives to gather more momentum, the religious authorities prepared a case against Him and had Him executed. Those in power have a habit of behaving in this way to silence those who offer alternative ways of making sense of the world.

Truth is contaminated by our urge for power and security. All of us, not just church leaders, are bound to this sin. Despite our best intentions, whilst ever we are caught up in power we are like carriers of a virus that saps the imagination that could generate the hope for a different future. But there are other reasons why we should be wary of accumulating power. Power in itself is neither a good nor a bad thing. Like the stories that form us, power has the capacity to be used for both good and ill. However, when we are powerful we heighten our potential for sin. Power, often when it takes the guise of money, has the ability to increase the speed at which an enterprise or a relationship corrupts or deteriorates. The lust for power expresses itself in deep and often unknowing allegiance to the powerful, which in turn leads to swapping the struggle for truth for the easy, engineered consensus associated with hegemony.

The way of Jesus, in demonstrating the viability of alternative values, makes clear that there are Kingdom values and processes that can up-end the hegemonic system that entraps us. These values and processes are the sinews of God's gracious economy.

Resistance to new ways of seeing

Having given theologians a tough time for their failure to articulate the dynamic of hegemony, let me turn the tables and tackle the intellectual resistance of sociologists. Despite the fact that sociology involves the study of the interactions of groups and societal patterns, sociologists resist naming the consistent dysfunction of humankind. It never ceases to amaze me that sociologists can do their work without at some stage being intrigued by the consistent and recurring sinfulness of human behaviour. Perhaps in the days of optimism, assumed progress and the loosening of inhibitions to talk of sin would have spoiled the party. However, in the more mellow and anxious times that are upon us, the concept of sin will soon be unfurled as a sociological category. This gap in sociological theorizing highlights that the search for understanding in a hegemonic smog is an endless struggle. It is not a case of unmasking once and for all the power(s) that are camouflaged and protected by the hegemonic order, for there is a continual contest taking place. This means that shaking off partisan perception in relation to one aspect of life serves to move us on to the next challenge to our taken-for-granted view of the world.

Thomas Kuhn coined the term *paradigm shift* in his book *The Structure of Scientific Revolutions*[8] and this represents one of the classic insights associated with the sociology of knowledge. Kuhn examines how scientific thinking is routinely shaped by what has gone before. Scientists, as in every occupational community, are inducted into thinking and seeing in accordance with an accepted body of knowledge. The rewards they receive and the sanctions they face ensure this. However, over time new insights emerge which challenge the accepted world view – and initially these insights will be fiercely resisted. A paradigm shift occurs when the new knowledge can demonstrate its capacity to explain all that the previous theory could as well as generate new insights.

Kuhn emphasizes the discomfort and even distress that is associated with these shifts in understanding, as vested interest is challenged and a new mode of thinking and understanding begins its reign. Kuhn's assessment of the process of scientific revolutions implies that *progress* is made in relation to our understanding – at least in relation to our theoretical understanding.[9] The parallels with the process of theological revolutions are significant, except that in its past, the Church's capacity to resist a paradigm shift was far more potent than that of the scientific community. The Church, after all, could bring death as well as eternal damnation upon those who dissented from orthodoxy.

The current struggle within the theological domain could be described as one between academic and committed theology: committed theology being the term used to describe *partisan* theology. However, in this instance the bias is in favour of the poor, because committed theology emerges from reading the Gospels from the perspective of the excluded. Liberation theology makes the case that where we are in the pecking order affects the way in which we see and understand the Gospel. In particular, when those who are poor or excluded read and reflect on the Bible, new insights and priorities emerge around familiar texts. From this, it becomes possible to see the previously unnoticed weaknesses within traditional Biblical exegesis. Traditional or academic theology, as well as the mainstream Church, has been unable to dismiss the legitimacy of reading the Gospels from the perspective of the poor; for when we do so, our capacity to make sense of Jesus' teaching and actions is significantly enhanced. As Kuhn indicates, when one theory can take account of all that the previous theory could explain, *and* has an additional explanatory capacity, then the scene is set for a paradigm shift.

The challenge to the Church is to decide whether these local theologies, as they are rather dismissively referred to by traditional Biblical scholars and theologians, do represent a paradigm shift that marks progress, rather than simply a difference in our understanding of the Gospel. The fact that they are described as local theologies illustrates one of the ruses of denial and defensiveness exercised by the mainstream or dominant theological community. For example, Harvey, having acknowledged that the hitherto shamefully neglected concept of liberation might be a key to theological understanding, finds it necessary to backtrack and dodge the implications of this. For he then gives an account of how traditional theologians 'Counter the radicalism of liberation theologies, by arguing, with some justice, that the situation in most "developed" countries was vastly different from that in Latin America, and that this theological approach had, at best, no more than local validity.'[10]

Harvey then goes on to announce that the real impact of such local theology is that 'It will never again be possible to assume that theological truth and theological reasoning is the possession of a single cultural milieu'.[11] So here we see a traditional biblical scholar and theologian ceding some ground to the 'new theological kid on the bloc', but not to the extent of acknowledging its primacy. Harvey accepts the relativity of our understanding, i.e. the sociological insight that how we see and understand is influenced by our context, and therefore acknowledges the validity and universality of our struggle for truth. Not everyone would be willing to cede even this in the way that Harvey does. Some would wish to continue to contest this, for it marks the watershed between the right-answerism of fundamentalism and the essentially questing approach which anticipates new insights. However, Harvey, having acknowledged this achievement of Liberation theology, only grants it *local* relevance rather than general – or catholic – relevance.

In writing in this manner Anthony Harvey illustrates the key points in the discussion here. He helpfully supports the overall point that claims to truth in the theological realm are not possible, but he also demonstrates the struggle for hegemonic power. Harvey's ambivalence in relation to the claims to validity of liberation theology is not just protecting the interests of established, academic theologians, he is also protecting those of us who benefit from the current global *status quo*. The traditional mode invariably finds safety in numbers so Harvey's defensive rationale appeals to the common sense that suits us in the Western world. Harvey maintains that the oppression which exists in non-Western countries is *local* or situational. This obscures the possibility that oppression in the non-Western world could be *structural*, i.e. due to established power relations in which some parties benefit at the cost of others, and that this process is expressed and reinforced by institutionalized procedures.[12] The point to note is that this undermining, or ignoring, of the more challenging interpretation is done without guile. Rather it is a product of the hegemonic smog which inhibits our ability to be radical and rigorous in relation to the assumptions which form the building blocks of our thinking.

Reclaiming Eve and the apple

If truth is something that has to be struggled for because of the impact of our context on our perception and understanding, then a second insight emerges, especially if we are prepared to acknowledge that such shaping is neither innocent nor random. The hegemonic order that defends and promotes the interests of established power is a manifestation of sin – original sin. To draw attention to this aspect of classic Christian doctrine sounds hopelessly old-fashioned. Alistair McFadyen explains why. He suggests that the idea that we should be held responsible for something that we do not consciously bring about is contrary to our moral hegemony. Furthermore, the notion of original sin is so caught up in the hard-to-believe Adam and Eve story, that it is easy to shrug off the theological concept that the story generates.[13]

Sin is a more radical and extensive dynamic than our rational world allows. The interference of sin in our thinking and seeing is not just random, it is directional. This direction is always to serve the interests of our anxious egos, and invariably this involves appeasing and pleasing the powerful. I return to the case notes that were written by the forerunners of today's social workers, and which condemned young women to live the rest of their lives in institutions for the morally defective. Their actions fall into the category that Jesus recognized as He was being nailed to the cross: our need for forgiveness because we know not what we do. For the matron of the Mother and Baby Home it would have been far easier to label the poor servant as morally defective than to challenge the seductive or aggressive capacity of the gentleman of the household. It would have been more than her job was worth to do that. She was acting in the way that her powerful board of governors had trained and encouraged her to do. I, and most people, in that context, would do the same. However, the sinful virus that affects us all is not just about following orders, it is about being frail, vulnerable people, who so often fail to perceive the wickedness of our actions, and if we can see our failure we are unlikely to have the guts to act on our perceptions. To me, this sounds like a good description of original sin, contemporized for the twenty-first century.

It is surely time to rehabilitate the story of Adam and Eve as a powerfully apt metaphor for the struggle for truth that marks our human existence. Adam and Eve, that embarrassing story that discredits the Bible in so many people's eyes, including many Christians, prefigures the sociological concept of hegemony. Eve's encounter with the snake provides an account of the essential dynamic at the heart of hegemony – the sin of sloth.[14] Harvey Cox observes that the first sin was not Eve eating the apple but rather Eve letting some snake tell her what to think and do. This first human sin in the Garden of Eden was not Eve eating of the tree of knowledge, as most people think, instead Harvey comments that the first sin was not such a Promethean feat: 'We do not defy the Gods by courageously stealing the fire from the celestial hearth, nothing so heroic. We fritter away our destiny by letting some snake tell us what to do.'[15] He concludes that the sin which Eve commits and Adam multiplies is the sin of sloth.

Sloth is one of the traditional seven deadly or capital sins, meaning that these sins generate a host of other specific sins. So the sin of sloth is not to be reduced to the idea of a lazy, come-day, go-day individual. It is far more potent. Sloth is the sin of accepting taken-for-granted perspectives on the world without question and without seeing them for what they are. Sloth involves turning our back on the need to think for ourselves and being unwilling to unravel the emotional investment we make in what normally passes for self-evident truths. Sloth was the original sin and it has dogged us since that snake hissed and smiled at Eve. Humankind has to own its perpetual vulnerability to be taken in by what passes as common sense. Common sense, which is lauded by the majority, is the route by which original sin passes unchallenged, for the most powerful ideologies are hidden from view precisely because they pass as common sense.

Jesus and original sin

Jesus, in taking on our human nature, also had to embrace both the partialness of understanding and the *partisan* nature of our perceptions that pass as common sense. The Son of God, born of Mary could not escape being contaminated by the common sense understandings of his culture. Jesus too had to do battle with the original sin of sloth. We can see this most clearly in the internal struggle that is provoked within him by the Syro-Phoenician woman. This unwelcome confrontation with a foreign woman illustrates how Jesus had to learn the importance of struggling for truth and shaking off the assumptions that had been formed within Him by the dominant culture of his day.

Jesus' encounter with the Syro-Phoenician woman is one of the most notable stories in the Gospels. It is told with slight variation in both Matthew 15 and Mark 7. The story is an awkward one for the preacher and theologian alike, for it portrays Jesus in a harsh light, and if we have the courage of modern-day convictions we have to acknowledge that we see Jesus acting in a racist way. The story goes as follows:

Jesus and his disciples had journeyed to the coastal region of Tyre. One suspects that He and the disciples were taking a break from their bruising time in Galilee. Anonymity was vital if they were to get the respite they needed. To everyone's annoyance and frustration, a woman arrived recognising Jesus and insisting that He heal her daughter. The disciples urged Jesus to 'Send her away, for she keeps shouting after us'. The woman had made such a commotion that the disciples feared that their cover would be blown. Her nuisance level reached such a pitch that she was eventually allowed to see Jesus. His first response was to subject her to verbal and racial abuse. He called her a dog because she was not a Jew, and He made clear that His ministry was first and foremost for the Jews: 'It is not fair to take the children's bread and throw it to the dogs,' said Jesus. The woman, perhaps the only person in the Gospels to use repartee to re-engage him, replied, 'Yes Lord, but even the dogs eat the crumbs that fall from the master's table'. We read that Jesus responded, 'Woman, great is your faith! Let it be done for you as you wish.'[16] When the woman returned home, she found her daughter healed.

Most theological effort in relation to this story focuses on a debate about Jesus seeing His ministry to the Gentiles taking place after the Jews, His own people, had accepted Him as the Messiah. The other response that the passage provokes is an attempt to minimize the offensiveness of Jesus' words to the woman. To call someone a dog, even today, is the supreme insult in the East. Many scholars alert us to the fact that in the Greek the term which is used is not dog, but a word for pup or puppies. This has the effect of turning the encounter into something more akin to friendly banter. But Nineham thwarts this idea by noting that, as far as Jesus' original words were concerned, neither Hebrew nor Aramaic have any linguistic form that corresponds with the words pups and puppies.[17]

The great challenge in this story is how to square the racial abuse which Jesus hands out to this non-Jewish woman, with the fundamental assumption that Jesus lived His life on earth without sin. We are faced with some tough options: either racial abuse is not a sin, or Jesus apparently did commit sin. However, there is a realistic and honourable way to resolve this dilemma, and it is rooted in the struggle that all of us have to free ourselves to think openly and to rise above the original sin of sloth. Jesus, in calling the woman a dog, was thinking and acting as His culture had conditioned Him to do. As Mary's son, brought up as a Jew in Nazareth, it would have been impossible for Him to do anything other than to think and act as a Jew. None of us, not even the incarnate Son of God, can escape the limitations and shaping forced upon us by the culture into which we are born, and in which we grow up. Jesus, in the encounter with the Syro-Phoenician woman, is demonstrating that even He did not have access to direct or uncontaminated experience of the world. In becoming our brother, Jesus, like each of us, absorbed the habits and limitations of seeing and thinking associated with the dominant culture in which we live.

Jesus thought and acted as a Jew when He was confronted by the persistence of this woman from Syro-Phoenicia. It is not a sin to have thoughts and attitudes which are a product of our cultural background. The sin which Jesus risked was to refuse to enter into dialogue with this woman, and thus miss the insight which she revealed. Jesus, by the grace of God, was engaged by the woman's refusal to trade insults with Him or to be deferential when confronted by elitist Judaism. Jesus was willing to be changed by this encounter, He was prepared to listen and learn from a stranger. Furthermore, He was open to the possibility of being changed and of altering His view of the world and His own priorities by the testimony of a Gentile woman.

The story demonstrates the speed and efficiency by which it is possible for us to see things afresh. Jesus did not change His ministry and mission as a result of long discussions and great heart searching. It happened as a result of a momentary encounter. However, that moment of insight can resonate through a lifetime and transform the cluster of values which make us who we are.

Jesus, in His incarnation, entered the realm of original sin and had to work hard to transcend its grip. For the powers that shape our seeing and thinking are always acting upon us. Jesus' encounter with the Syro-Phoenecian woman and the way this transformed His understanding and future actions emphasizes the epistemological significance of an encounter with strangers. It also reinforces the importance of opportunities to journey out from our 'known' world to that which challenges us and shakes up our taken-for-granted view of the world. Jesus required a gracious encounter with a foreigner to alert Him to the sinful limitations of His assumptions. Our journey towards truth advances not so much when we are in the company of the likeminded but when we are in the company of those who see things differently from us. The gift of the multicultural and multifaith environment that we now inhabit means that such accompaniment is to hand.

We have to be content with only ever having a partisan understanding of the Gospel, because our understanding is always inhibited and contaminated by our culture, as Jesus came to realize. We always, in this life, will see through a glass dimly. Our Islamic brothers and sisters also recognize this struggle. Alongside the concept of *jihad*, which has entered our everyday vocabulary, Islam also has the concept of *ijtihad*, which is the obligation of the Moslem to exercise intellectual effort in the pursuit of truth. Whilst *jihad* has come to mean holy struggle in the sense of war, *ijtihad* means struggle or effort in the cause of truth. This is something that we all need to embrace, for no longer can we pretend that our perceptions are reliable. Truth is something to be struggled for and never to be grasped. We have to journey towards truth and that journey never ends.

In our history, the Church has operated as if it was in full possession of all understanding. The parallel is, of course, with the Pharisees and the way they behaved in Jesus' day. This is shame enough for most Christians, however, the claim to be in full possession of understanding carries a second jeopardy in a post-modern context. In a post-modern culture any institution which presents itself as having authority because of its possession of understanding will be regularly and thoroughly undermined. In a post-modern world it is wiser to exchange power for authenticity.

Notes

1 John 18.38.
2 For details of this research see David Hay and Ann Morisy 'Secular Society/Religious Meanings: A Contemporary Paradox' in *The Review of Religious Research* 26(3) 213–27 and David Hay, *Exploring Inner Space* (London: Mowbray, 1987).
3 Raymond Williams, *Problems in Materialism and Culture* (London: New Left Books/Verso, 1980).
4 Sixty years on, in that Midlands town there remained two wards in a nearby hospital that were full of elderly women who had been categorized as morally defective. The length of time they had spent in hospital and the shamefulness of the label morally defective meant that they had become so institutionalized that they were unable to cope with moving back into the community and normal society.
5 I write in the past tense because the current preoccupation with post-modernity involves debate about whether there is any longer a dominant culture. The fragmentation associated with post-modernity makes us far more difficult to police because each of us marches to a different tune. We have the option of buying into one or another value system or none at all. This means that those of us who opt for a Christian foundation to our lives are not just powerless but judged as irrelevant to the majority.
6 A good example of this is the Road Peace Movement. Those associated with Road Peace make a point of using the expression 'road incidents', because very few of the

incidents that occur on the road are *accidents*, invariably someone is responsible for them.

7 Luke 1.46–55.

8 Thomas S. Kuhn, *The Structure of Scientific Revolutions* (Chicago: University of Chicago Press, 1962).

9 Kuhn's work is confident that progress in relation to our understanding of the world is feasible. However, the hegemony which formed Kuhn's view when he was writing would not have enabled him to identify the significance of distinguishing between progress in theoretical understanding and progress associated with the technological developments associated with these gains in theoretical understanding. The current hegemonic contest involves the recognition of the double-edged nature of technological gains and the often unanticipated disruption this can cause. Our post-modern mentality enables us to query whether technological progress is progress at all. Such questioning and hesitation would have been completely alien to Kuhn writing in the 1960s.

10 Anthony Harvey, *By What Authority* (London: SCM Press, 2001), p. 11.

11 Ibid., p. 11.

12 The way we categorize the prevalence of oppression is significant. To suggest that oppression is local or situational implies that it is the product of a specific context which enables onlookers to distance themselves, unless they are moved by some personal compassion. This view of oppression is characteristic of liberalism. It is also possible to view oppression as endemic, suggesting that it is dangerous and liable to spread. In this instance it is advantageous to the onlooker to act before they find themselves caught up in the process. To categorize oppression as structural suggests that there is no escaping the process because it is a basic feature of human life to which we have to be constantly alert – and ultimately rescued from. This is the classic Christian understanding

which often gets corrupted into a view that having once been rescued we are no longer in danger of the process of oppression and being oppressors.

13 Alistair McFadyen, *Bound To Sin* (Cambridge: Cambridge University Press, 2000), p. 21.

14 I have made the case for sloth as a pernicious virus, and also for how Jesus had to struggle with the danger of sloth in my book *Beyond the Good Samaritan* (London: Mowbray, 1997). I repeat it here because I consider it to be a fundamental insight for Christians today in our struggle for truth.

15 Harvey Cox, (1968) *On Not Leaving It To The Snake* (London, SCM Press, 1968), p. xiv.

16 Matthew 15.21-8. Quotations taken from the New Revised Standard Version Bible (Cambridge: Cambridge University Press, 1989).

17 D. E. Nineham, *Saint Mark* (London; Penguin Books, 1963).

7

The Explicit Domain

When the Church was at its full Christendom power people went to church and people believed what they heard in church, or at least if they didn't believe what they heard they would certainly think twice before saying so. The explicit teaching of the Church had status and people expected to receive a direct and systematic presentation of the formularies of the Christian faith from the pulpit. The expectations that have prevailed for centuries have dissolved in 50 years and the venerable structures and habits of our churches have been marooned on a tiny island of the faithful. The change has been so rapid it is debilitating as the old structures prove too costly to be maintained by the remnant. But grief is compounded because of the repeated failure to engage with anything but the faithful few.[1] This difficulty is compounded because of the problem of charting a path that can take into account the vagaries of a fragmented culture. In the face of such fragmentation within the wider world there has been no rationale available to the Church that can provide sufficient incentive to reassess and reorganize how resources are deployed. The doldrums that becalm a weakening Church are as much to do with the fragmentation of the wider society as they are to do with any resistence to change.

The challenge is to our imagination. Is it possible to chart an approach that relates to our shared humanity and can connect with people at a level that is deeper than the post-modern habits and assumptions that dominate our lives? I should like to offer a chart that tries to do his. The map that I offer has three domains:

♦ the explicit domain;
♦ the foundational domain;
♦ the vocational domain.

(The foundational and vocational domains will be considered in the following chapters.)

Those who go to church Sunday by Sunday will be most familiar with the *explicit* domain. Most of our church practice is geared up to the explicit domain, which is characterized by public worship, organized around the formularies of the Christian faith, and shaped by the diverse but explicit expressions of particular churchmanship and denomination. In the days of Christendom, it made sense to deploy resources to ensure a systematic presentation of an equally systematic faith. In fact, in the days of Christendom, when Christian belief and practice dominated people's world view, there appeared to be little need for the Church to do anything else.

The explicit domain is not just a case of maintaining theological orthodoxy and ecclesiastical orthodoxy, it is about recruiting or *forming* recruits to be adept in relation to these orthodoxies. Each denomination has different practices to ensure that the nuances of the denomination are transferred intact to their recruits. However, whilst these explicit expressions of faith may be very clear to their adherents, in a post-Christendom and post-Christian context, they are obscure to the vast majority outside the denomination. Those of us inside the churches may make sense and find coherence in the explicit domain: for most others, the explicit domain is experienced as a dense, exclusive culture. The explicit domain is characterized by impenetrable symbols and pro-cedures which make it impossible to anticipate being able to participate or to have a fulfilling experience. The explicit domain – which is the routine of church life – presents a threshold that is too high for most people to feel they can cross it. I find a parallel in my experience of classical music:

> I remember when Classic FM first hit the sound waves. I heard music that I had never heard before; I found it very attractive and appealing. Unfortunately it was impossible and remains impossible, for me to share the pleasure that comes from such listening. The reason for my silence, and my isolation, and the difficulty of participating and partaking more of classical music, is that I do not have the language, or conceptual framework, that goes with classical music. I do attend classical concerts, but only risk clapping when others lead the way. I learned this essential the embarrassing way. I practise looking knowingly and nod sagely in the interval conversation in order to hide the petrifying fear that someone might ask me what I thought of the contralto.
>
> Part of my difficulty is that I know that classical music is full of technical terms. I know that there are symphonies, concertos, codas and librettos. However, I neither know what each of these mean nor do I know how to form a sentence using such concepts. I know I can't use colloquial words like tune, beat, song or lyrics without looking an oaf. So I stay silent, maintaining self-exclusion, because of lack of confidence about entering the explicit domain that surrounds classical music.

I expose my ignorance about classical music[2] in order to illustrate the difficulty that the explicit domain of church life can hold for many people. We have made the explicit domain so complex and so inaccessible that people are doubly anxious about partaking of it. To the non-adept access to God via our established churches seems so peppered with obscure concepts that they become disabled. When should they refer to Jesus? Or should they say Christ or is that a swear word? And is the Son of God the same as God, and who precisely is the child of God? Add to this the business of bowing heads and sitting and standing, it is a bold person indeed who enters the explicit domain in an attempt to give expression to what is coming to birth in their soul.

The significance of symbols

There is an additional problem in relation to the explicit domain and it is a very tough one. The fact that Christian symbolism has faded from our culture presents us with a serious challenge. The tricky business of symbols often gets coalesced into a more straightforward issue: lack of familiarity. The response to this is to assume that we now have to make a point of introducing people to the significance of the symbols that are so essential to the explicit domain of church life. By osmosis or growing familiarity, and occasionally by direct teaching we hope that people will begin to understand the significance of bread, wine and even the image of a man in the agonies of death hanging on a cross. However, to assume the difficulty with our symbols is just a case of lack of familiarity is to underestimate just how tricky the problem is.

There are two tough problems associated with the symbols that are so central to the explicit domain. The first difficulty is that people might be *repulsed* by the things we do in church. Insights in relation to this dreadful problem are available from the social anthropologist George Herbert Mead, and sociologists such as Howard Becker and Ervine Goffman. These writers emphasize how communication and interaction between people are dependent on the way in which they understand the symbols that each is using. Symbols, in this instance, include language, actions and mannerisms. Effective communication requires people to share the same symbols and to understand the symbols in the same way, or to be able to negotiate a shared understanding. This process Mead and others refer to as symbolic interactionism.

In a fragmented society such as our own, such agreement around symbols is the exception rather than the norm. Furthermore, unlike in the past, there is little sanction imposed on people to negotiate a shared understanding. It has become acceptable and even cool to maintain an idiosyncratic, symbolic system. A good example of this is the use of the word *gay*. Some have taken umbrage that the delightful innocence of the word has been contaminated by its use by the homo-sexual community as their mnemonic for the 1970s' motto: Good As You. However, more recently schoolchildren have adopted the term 'gay' to indicate something that is naff or of profound bad taste. Symbolic interactionism does not imply that people will be willing to shed their particular usage and understanding, rather it warns us that meanings attached to symbols can be, and increasingly are, contested.

We misunderstand the situation if we think it simply a case of the symbols that dominate the explicit domain being *unfamiliar* to those outside the Church. They are very familiar. I think in particular of the Eucharist. To invite people to partake of the blood and body of Jesus is to the hearer who is shaped by the wider culture akin to some kind of macabre expression of primitive behaviour. It chimes in with witch-craft or devil worship. We might protest at such an interpretation, but the cultural influences that dominate our understanding of such symbols are now more prevalent and potent than those of our distant Christian heritage. In today's context our traditional and most holy symbols do not travel well. Blood is now about contamination, it carries AIDS, the sharing of the single cup is seen as foolish and cultic, and drinking blood is the characteristic of Dracula and other fang-bearing creatures. It is a big ask to expect people to cast off the resonances that now dominate and contaminate our precious symbols. In Mead's terms the scope for *effective* symbolic interactionism becomes less and less likely.

On Ash Wednesday 2003, the war against Saddam Hussein in Iraq was beginning to gain momentum. The mood across the nation was very sombre. There were a significant number of new faces in the congregation, perhaps taking advantage of an open church in order to reflect on the heaviness of the moment and their hearts. They found themselves partaking of the solemn symbolism of Ash Wednesday. Everyone in the church walked to the chancel and allowed, and perhaps even welcomed, the priest putting ash on their brow and having the powerful words 'Remember you are dust, and to dust you shall return, turn to Christ and repent of your sins' said to them in the process of their ashing. The ancient rite travelled well and fitted the mood. The talk of dust being of the moment, as they (and we, the regulars at the church) remembered the dust storms that had featured on the early evening news, and had already become a signature of the war in Iraq.

The symbol of the ash and the remembrance of our own fragility and insignificance fitted the mood of the time because people's symbols could interact without interference. The symbols offered through the explicit domain provided a ready fit with where people were at, and the experience was profound. Here was the Church doing what only it could do.

The next sequence in that Ash Wednesday liturgy travelled less well. The second invitation that was issued by the priest was to receive the body and blood of Jesus that was given for us. Those who had come through the doors for solace declined this invitation. They remained in their seats and watched the regulars move to the front of the church. This was the point when the cultic dominated rather than the shared sense of vulnerability. No longer did our symbols interact effectively with those from outside.

We are naive if we persist in thinking that the difficulty with our explicit domain is just that of obscurity. The situation is more challenging than this: only a few of our symbols can rise above the negative associations that they have come to carry in our post-Christian environment. Added to this there is a second difficulty associated with the symbolic nature of our church life.

Ronald Rolheiser[3] suggests that the scientific capacity to explain so many aspects of our lives and experiences means that fewer and fewer aspects of life get encompassed by symbols. So much of what we encounter now can be explained in mundane or routine ways. This ability to manipulate and dominate our environment, and our preoccupation with it, has resulted in a depleted *symbolic repertoire*. Our need for symbols has diminished in relation to everyday life because we have access to quasi-explanatory idioms. Such earthbound and functional use of language does not lift our eyes to a horizon which speaks of the holy or the *set apart*. No longer do the words we use point us to or link us with the mystery of life. In fact they do the very opposite. They cause us to gravitate towards the functional and commonplace. *High* symbols,[4] on the other hand, allude to the sacred, signify *the more* in life that is only partially knowable and point to the mystery of life.

The high symbols of days gone by continually linked us to God and acknowledged God's involvement in the world. In contrast, the current dominant expressive mode, that of low, earthbound symbols, indicates the predominance of a very different world view: our day-to-day experiences are a series of sensations that *belong to us* and they are part of a world that can be *taken for granted*. This lack of recognition, and even denial, of the mystery or sacredness of life has a host of repercussions. On a profound and practical level one suspects it has an impact on the way in which we treat, and *expend*, the natural environment. On a more prosaic level it means that artistic creation has nowhere else to go other than take us further and further into the mundane. So the artist, Tracey Emin, invites us to look and linger at her unmade bed, and more than a decade before, we were invited to ponder the pile of bricks that claimed centre stage at Tate Britain. We are entertained by earthbound poetry and gangsta rap and holy days are degraded into bank holidays. The result is that the sacred or the holy evaporates from our consciousness. This means that it is not just our awareness of God that gets snuffed out, so too do our routes to God.

Secularism reduces all aspects of our lives to the mundane. As more and more aspects of our lives are manipulated by human enterprise this squeezes out the possibility of the holy or sacred. A secular world view or mindset insists that this world, and this life, is all there is. Rolheiser comments that 'We wake up in this world as orphans, all on our own ... ordinary experience does not contain traces of ultimacy or set us against a divine horizon.'[5] However, he goes on to protest that although the dominant culture urges upon us this secular world view, people do not experience themselves or their lives in this way. He suggests that although our routine habits might indicate the dominance of secularism 'There are traces of ultimacy[6] in ordinary experience, [however], we stop short of appropriating them. Moreover, we do in fact feel God, we are just not aware enough of what we are feeling ... our normal experience appears to us as purely secular because we are not sufficiently contemplative within it.'[7] So although the domination of low symbols only allows reference to the mundane, there remains within our deepest being an inkling that there is more to life than meets the eye. However, the constrained and low symbolic repertoire that we possess does not encourage contemplation of *the more* that exists beyond the mundane.

The earthbound symbols that populate our linguistic codes do not encourage us to lift our eyes and sense the holy or to recognize the felt presence of God that is potentially ours – and which is the foundation of worship. This is an immense challenge to a church which invests so heavily in the explicit domain. In a materialistic, earthbound culture we have to do prior work before people can contemplate the presence of God, let alone worship.

The need to create a foundation

This prior work belongs to the foundational domain. This constrained symbolic repertoire presents a new agenda to the Church: to give priority to fostering the dimly perceived and rarely articulated awareness of the holy. Never before has the Church had to embark on the task of re-enchanting our view of the world. Now, when so many of our resources are devoted to the explicit domain, we have to regroup in order to attend to the challenge of helping people to have confidence in their inkling that we do not live by bread alone, and that there is more to life than meets the eye.

Responding to this challenge is made more difficult by the

fact that the explicit domain claims most of the Church's resources. Our past inebriation with power has meant that the Church has concentrated her resources on the explicit domain. Virtually all the formal training that is available through our churches aims at equipping people to function in the explicit domain. Our imagination is dominated, or should I say limited, by the habits that belong to the explicit domain. Furthermore, in relation to the explicit domain we have developed a pathology which makes change hard to achieve. We have become prone to:

♦ focusing on the organization rather than its environment;
♦ overvaluing our past methods and commitments compared to new ones;
♦ narrowing the intake of information from the outside world;
♦ a degeneration of the steering or coordinating capacity of the Church hierarchy, that especially involves overvaluing structure rather than function;
♦ aiming for near-to-hand objectives rather than the longer-term goal;
♦ investing in current structures and preferences rather than those which will involve fundamental change.[8]

This characterization of pathology is provided by Karl Deutsch. However, Deutsch wasn't writing about the Church, he was concerned with politics, and the characterization he provides relates to governments and the pathology that overtakes them when they have held office for a long time. In his book *The Nerves of Government* he concludes that political theory must take seriously the *eternal insufficiency of man*[9] if our corporate enterprises are to withstand the corrupting overestimations such as those above. The corruption or drift from the real purpose of the organization is, according to Deutsch, almost inevitable. However, he suggests that a self-governing organization can withstand and even rise above these pathologies by:

- heeding the need for humility to counteract pride;
- embracing faith and commitment to counteract luke-warmness;
- allowing reverence to replace idolatry;
- taking seriously the reality of grace.[9]

Let me stress that in making the case for these health-giving strategies Deutsch is writing as a political theorist. He is commending to other political scientists the effectiveness of spiritual disciplines in ensuring organizational viability and longevity. There is deep encouragement for us here.

I remind you of the opening paragraphs of the first chapter of this book. It was to recall that the Diocese in which I worked became a *self-governing organization* in 604 AD. We are well familiar with the spiritual disciplines that Deutsch commends to governments and politicians. Over the last 1,400 years no doubt there will have been many occasions when the Church will have had to have heeded such spiritual disciplines, for there is no other way to explain such extraordinary longevity. We need to remind ourselves that by the application of the spiritual disciplines commended by Deutsch the rigidity associated with our overinvestment in the explicit domain will liquefy. Energy will then be able to flow fulsomely into the other domains that have become critical to the task of upholding our faith effectively in a world that has become taken for granted and mundane.

Notes

1 We need to be wary about getting too downcast about church attendance. Churches are still the most significant voluntary activity in Britain. Although numbers have fallen hugely the number of people participating in any voluntary activity has plummeted over the last twenty years. This is why the issue of social capital and the associated weakening of civil society is causing so much concern.

2 My embarrassment about my ignorance has been eased by the following comments by Andrew Clark, the music critic at the *Financial Times*, 'Classical music will be marginalized if it does not make efforts to embrace a wider public ... the evidence of Classic FM is that millions 'listen to it just because they like the sound, even if they don't know the name of the piece being played.' Clark speculates whether the aristocratic art form of classical music can ever flourish in our microwave, mass culture. The issues he raises parallel some of those we face as Church: 'Most people still find the barrier too high between acquaintance with great composers' music and crossing the threshold of a concert hall ... the rituals of performance make them uneasy, or they are put off by archaic programme formulas ... 65 per cent of six- to 14-year-olds in a recent UK survey were unable to name a single classical composer. ... By the end of the twentieth century, the classical music industry had become a cultural dinosaur. ... It is not just classical music that is facing a crisis of confidence. The trend towards shallowness and superficiality is a general threat. ... For the first time classical music will have to undertake missionary work ...' (*FT Weekend*, 5/6 April 2003).

3 Ronald Rolheiser, *The Shattered Lantern* (New York: Crossroad, 1997).

4 Rolheiser uses the expressions *low and high symbolic hedges* (p. 49). I find this terminology unhelpful because in this usage the idea of hedge is not that of separation but of a platform, i.e. a high symbolic hedge is one which alludes to God and the sacred, whereas a low symbolic hedge keeps our focus earthbound.

5 Ibid., pp. 124–5.

6 Are you a user of Microsoft Word? You probably are. Type the word *ultimacy* and you will find it appears underlined in red. Ultimacy is a word unrecognized by the spell checker. The ever-present spell checker wants to replace it with the word *intimacy*. The lack of recognition of a

word like ultimacy is a further example of the denuding of our repertoire of high symbols with which to enfold our experience.

7 Rolheiser, op. cit., p. 121.
8 These points are presented in slightly adapted form from those identified by Karl W. Deutsch in his book *The Nerves of Government* (London: The Free Press of Glencoe, 1963), pp. 223–8.
9 Ibid., p. 219.
10 Ibid., pp. 229–40.

8

The Foundational Domain

The practice of apologetics was once the chief means by which the Church encouraged people to embrace an explicit or systematic understanding of the Gospel and the practices of the Church. Apologetics is essentially an intellectual activity around which the Christian aims to present 'This is how I see it from a Christian perspective', and goes on to add, 'Can you not see it this way as well?' Apologetics was the chief response to the questioning that began with the Enlightenment and the scepticism that has gained momentum ever since. Added to scepticism is the anti-authoritarianism which both undermines churches as hierarchical institutions and the possibility of people being instructed in what to believe, this, as well as the low level of religious literacy adds to our difficulties. In such a context, harnessing apologetics as our main strategy for mission is not enough: other approaches need to be developed.

The Church has already begun to explore new approaches, particularly in response to the low level of religious literacy in Britain. These approaches need now to be categorized more closely. As part of this process of categorizing or mapping I wish to develop and outline the approaches associated with the *foundational domain*. In this domain the task is to work or engage with people to build their confidence in the intimations they have of an enduring reality and the non-material aspects of life. Work in the foundational domain could be described as 'A ministry of awakening, helping people to see beyond the daily round of worldly commitment, to awaken in them a sense of their eternal origin and destiny.'[1] So writes John O'Donohue. This has never been required before. But now, in response to the impact of secularization, we have to develop a ministry of recognition, i.e. helping people to *recognize* and name their sense of God, as well as encourage an acquaintance with the divine. Without fostering this recognition and valuing of the non-material aspects of life there is no foundation upon which to nurture faith.

The Roman Catholic Church in Ireland, recognizing that the spectre of child abuse will contaminate all encounters for a number of generations,[2] has become very aware of the prior work that now has to be done before people can engage with the explicit domain of faith and Church life. O'Donohue, writing with deep awareness of the poisoned environment in which priests now have to minister, beseeches his fellow priests to journey out into the terrain which I refer to as the foundational domain. He writes, 'Now that the constituency of religious practice is shrinking, the priesthood needs to have the courage to open the conversation of Spirit precisely in those areas where ideology, structures and personnel see nothing at all in the spiritual perspective.'[3] This challenge is also one that is familiar to those in chaplaincy work, perhaps in a hospital, an airport or a college. Although they may invest time in the explicit domain, the main focus of their efforts will be taking the 'courage to open the conversation of Spirit', to use O'Donohue's words, with those who do not share the same symbolic understandings as they do and do not have access to the high, symbolic repertoire that fosters a link with the holy or transcendent aspects of our world.

In the foundational domain, there has to be a natural, unforced hospitality to all areas and kinds of experience. If people are to allow their imagination to form and shape the *possibility* of God they need to be free from the fear of censure. Chaplains, perhaps more than other ministers, have to develop the skill of code switching. This means listening to the sentiment being expressed however inadequately and unorthodoxly, and then being willing to *meet* that sentiment respectfully and to resist the urge to shape or force that sentiment to fit with Christian orthodoxy. Perhaps a conceptual or theological tool can be offered that might enable the person to ponder their experience or attitude more deeply, or provide reassurance that the intuition the person has is all that is needed in acknowledging the presence of God in their struggle. If the chaplain has the opportunity to pray with a person it is an opportunity to enfold the person with words that are part of the high, symbolic repertoire that gives access to the holy, lifting the person beyond the mundane. The chaplain works at the level of the imagination. The task is to help people see beyond the routine, mundane consciousness of everyday life and discover that within our ordinary experiences there are rumours of angels and traces of ultimacy.

Chaplaincy is not the only arena where work in relation to the foundational domain is taken seriously.[4] This is terrain that is likely to be familiar to many of the community initiatives that churches have developed, particularly in neighbourhoods with multiple deprivation.

A parish in North London worked hard to ensure they had the resources to employ a part-time Children's Worker. Each year she, in turn, would fund-raise for the summer programme of events. The first priority was to book a visit to Regent's Park outdoor theatre. Her rationale was that it was vital to enliven the children's imagination if they were ever to explore faith in God. If they could not conceive of a world within a world in the way that theatre gives us practice, then the possibility of there being a God, who calls them His children, and knows them by name becomes so, so difficult. Her case was that in an area of severe social deprivation, the children might miss out on events that provoke imagination and encourage awareness that reality is a complex and creative phenomenon. If children are to sense that there is more to life than meets the eye then it helps if they have had the experience not just of being entertained but of entering another world, in a way that theatre is a regular signifier.[5]

Traditional evangelism has been about encouraging and helping people to relate to God. The task of the foundational domain is one step removed from this. The aim of our work in the foundational domain is to enable people to embrace *the possibility of God*. An implicit assumption of the foundational domain is that people have a deep capacity for sensing God. This goes back to Aquinas's theory of *adaequatio*. This theory maintains that a person needs to have some inner capacity to receive what is to be known if knowledge is to result from the encounter. In other words the capacity of the knower must be adequate to the thing to be known. Enlivening the inner capacity that allows the possibility of God and the possibility of God relating to each person is the essential challenge of the foundational domain. This means awakening within people the capacity to be astonished and be surprised by *the more* in life. Fostering people's imagination is essential to the foundational domain because the aim is to prepare the ground for the tall story of the incarnation of God into the world, for this is a non-negotiable aspect of the explicit domain.

In the past, the aesthetics associated with Church and faith helped people to escape from the niggling interference of our overly rational and earthbound minds. Art, architecture and music have been the method of engaging with people and helping them to acquire a high symbolic repertoire that equips them for the explicit domain. However, the ear and eye shaped by popular culture is likely to find the traditional aesthetic of Church far too highbrow for comfort.[6] The challenges of the foundational domain require other ways of helping people to lift themselves (or be lifted) out of a humdrum perspective on life. Churches now need to engage with people through the skills and gifts of a community poet, writer or an artist in residence. Here, in a participative way, people can be given permission to express their inner perceiving. There is opportunity to learn from each other, and to be surprised and delighted by the beauty and coherence of what results. By harnessing the resources of imagination, creativity, conviviality and the expertise of community artists, spiritual awareness that is muted can be expressed more fully.

Attitude as well as knowledge

Those who have researched patterns of church attendance draw a distinction between those who are 'lapsed' church attenders and those who have never been involved.[7] Research suggests that churches are far more successful at coaxing the lapsed back to church than they are at attracting those who have never been involved. There may be two reasons for this: our inclination to keep persisting in engaging people in the explicit domain of Sunday by Sunday church and our concentration on the knowledge dimension, i.e. trying to encourage people to *know more* about the Gospel. There may be theological reasons why our aim should be to improve people's knowledge of our Christian teaching, however, to invest all our efforts in this form of outreach does little to address the *attitudinal* problems that people have with the Church.

Our work in relation to the foundational domain has to engage with people's *attitude* towards God, religion and the Church rather than working with people in relation to the tenets of the Christian faith. Recent and welcome developments such as the Alpha and Emmaus courses have done much to help people get more knowledge about what is at the heart of our Christian faith. However, for many the real issue is an attitude problem with the Church and religion. My hunch is that it is inappropriate to tackle the issue of negative attitudes to the Church[8] head-on. This does not mean ignoring the issue but it does mean being patient and persistent. It also calls for much greater emphasis on authenticity than in the past, and this has to be achieved against the constant undermining drone of the media. There are, however, occasional opportunities that come to our aid in relation to the task of rehabilitating the Church in people's eyes. There are occasions when people need something that links heaven and earth, and apt liturgy has the capacity to do this.

Apt liturgy

Apt liturgy is about the churches doing what only they can do.[9] It is an art that churches are becoming increasingly adept at expressing. Apt liturgy is a very valuable resource in relation to the foundational domain because it is short and simple, and often can take place in mundane environments. Apt liturgy does not require people to cross the threshold of the church. Furthermore, apt liturgy as a tool for working in relation to the foundational domain spares us worry about *dumbing down*, which tends to be a recurring anxiety around family services. Apt liturgy is specifically about wide accessibility and (usually) engaging with people who are having to deal with hard emotions.

The first instance of apt liturgy that I encountered took place in a minibus. Members of the Seniors' Club had planned a summer trip to revisit the places to which they had been evacuated during the war. The minister recognized that this provided an opportunity to offer high symbols that could engage with their experience, which no doubt would be characterized by all kinds of complex emotions: gratitude for today being able to live in peace and not war; revitalized by happy memories but disappointed by a community that no longer expressed the solidarity born of struggle; saddened by the loss of loved ones yet gratified that the family had held together through thick and thin; troubled by a world that despite the optimism at the end of the war didn't seem to have got any better. The minister having recognized the possible range of emotions then had to rise to the challenge of encompassing such diverse and potent emotions in less than eight minutes.[10]

The occasions for apt liturgy are often characterized by an emotional struggle. Therefore the priest[11] must not evade emotion but be able to name it in such a way that extends people's understanding and generates reassurance. This reassurance comes from linking the particular struggle or distress with more universal but related struggles. For example, for the Seniors' Club returning in their minibus, the minister made links between the warfare of 50 years before that engulfed London, and the experience of war faced by nations today. Apt liturgy in relation to a project providing debt advice might link the personal debt of those seeking advice with the debt faced by the poor nations of the world. This emphasizes the fraternal relations that exist not just with those who are nearby but with those in other parts of the world, as well as with those of past generations. The reassurance generated by apt liturgy comes from emphasizing that we are not alone or unique in our struggle, there is solidarity with others, as well as God's solidarity with us His children.

Part of the art of apt liturgy is to indicate or acknowledge God's involvement in these universal struggles as well as His concern for each individual. This capacity to signify God's incarnation or presence in the world is one of the essential tasks of the foundational domain. It is not sufficient just to encourage recognition of there being more to life than meets the eye: if a foundation is to be prepared for the explicit or essential aspects of our faith then God cannot remain a distant, uninvolved power or force. Apt liturgy therefore has to express or allude to the intimacy or alongsideness of God who is our Heavenly Father. So, for example, the minister providing the apt liturgy on the minibus concluded her prayers by thanking God for His son Jesus, who also died for the sake of others. The minister who created the apt liturgy for the debt advice project concluded his prayers by thanking God, who through Jesus His Son waived everyone's debts.

Apt liturgy should not be confused with worship. Apt liturgy aims to take those who only half believe into special account. Worship is hard to achieve when the head is buzzing about whether one really believes in the orthodoxies of the Church. Apt liturgy is for those who only half believe or have inchoate beliefs, but recognize their need for reassurance, encouragement and courage. In preparing the ground for the explicit domain, which most certainly does involve worship, apt liturgy concentrates on achieving:

♦ memories of the heart, i.e. ideas and images that can be pondered;
♦ enabling people to cope, especially when they are close to being overwhelmed by emotion;
♦ providing symbols or codes that 'waft us heavenward'.

Essentially, apt liturgy involves the thoughtful introduction of symbols that resonate with people's struggle. However these symbols must be neither too obscure nor too cultic if they are to help people to lift their eyes to a Godly horizon. The symbolic challenge is not difficult once we acknowledge that this is the primary issue that we have to address. The art is to locate a symbol that is not too hot, not too weird, but just right. Symbols of bread, water, nails, ash and even a nappy pin are able to be shared effectively between people. Our imagination rarely fails, and when it does falter we can be confident that copious lighting of candles[12] provides an unfailing corporate focus.

The real challenge in relation to apt liturgy is recognizing, and having the confidence to seize the moment, especially as that moment may be one that is linked with pain and grief, as most occasions for apt liturgy are likely to be associated with communal distress. The example of the Church's role in Soham in Cambridgeshire is characteristic of apt liturgy. The trauma of two young girls being murdered provided the local church with the challenge of doing what only it could: to give the community access to the Church's substantial repertoire of high symbols in order to provide succour in their intense distress.

Very often, to be alert to the scope for apt liturgy requires a foundation of community involvement by key players in the local church. Only by consistent networking, i.e. by determinedly journeying out, can the Church be alert to the struggles that people face, and achieve a level of trust sufficient for people to respond to an invitation to partake of apt liturgy. When working on the attitude dimension one cannot minister with platitudes from outside. Real conversation has to have taken place consistently with those who are alienated, post-religious or indifferent if a foundation is to be laid upon which to begin the work of disclosing the stifled traces of the divine presence.

Apt liturgy calls for emotional literacy because those who create and lead apt liturgy have to identify and relate to the immediate and raw emotions that beset people. The concept of emotional literacy should not be dismissed too hastily as psychobabble. Emotional literacy involves:

♦ the ability to understand and be in touch with one's own emotions;
♦ the ability to listen to and empathize with other people's emotions;
♦ the ability to express emotion.

Whilst emotional literacy is challenging enough in relation to individuals, apt liturgy calls for the ability to read how emotions can operate at the level of groups and even communities, *and then* having the confidence to go public on the basis of one's perceptions. Apt liturgy takes guts – as well as emotional literacy. It also requires the ability to articulate the dominant emotions in a manner which neither colludes nor indulges, but links people with abiding or eternal constructs. The commitment to embark on such a challenging task needs to be rooted in the twin convictions that tough emotions easily fester if they are not surfaced and that when the going gets tough people know their need for God.

Apt liturgy acknowledges people's emotional needs but also offers them related concepts and symbols. Very often, it is the stories that Jesus tells, or stories drawn from His life, that provide the resources for this process. The stories of

Jesus, because of His affinity to those who were vulnerable or excluded, resonate so strongly with the hard or difficult situations that call for apt liturgy. This inclusion of Bible stories can help heal the rift that has developed between people's spiritual intuitions and formal religion and the Church. One of the aims of the foundational domain is to provide people with a story about Jesus that they find themselves pondering in their hearts in the days that follow.

Effective apt liturgy provides people with new concepts and a new perspective on their struggle and distress. It also gives an intimation of hope. This combination of insight and hope may be very powerful. O'Donohue comments that 'Some of the most decisive moments in one's life are when someone shows you a new frontier and helps you across into a world of new possibility and promise. To be helped towards a new way of seeing is to be given access to a new world. At its highest point of intensity and possibility Meister Eckhart refers to this as the Birth of God in the Soul.'[13] This birthing of God in the soul is the very aim of the missionary task associated with the foundational domain, and apt liturgy is one of the most precise tools we have to enable this process.

As well as giving prominence to God's involvement in the world and in people's struggles, apt liturgy can also help sensitize people to sin. Sin cannot be ducked if people are to be able to respond to the non-negotiable elements of the explicit domain. The recognition of the nature of sin is needed before Jesus of Nazareth can become Jesus our Saviour. Whilst it may be inappropriate to try and achieve an acknowledgement of our sinfulness when a community is traumatized or distressed, apt liturgy prepared in response to communal grievances can heighten awareness of the sinful dynamics that dog us personally, communally and institutionally. Furthermore, having helped people to recognize sin, an opportunity is also created for acknowledging and sharing symbols of forgiveness.

Although apt liturgy is part of our work in the foundational domain some of the components will mirror those used in the explicit domain. For example, apt liturgy will probably involve:

♦ Identifying an occasion where Jesus and His stories meet our story, i.e. providing a story from the Gospels that resonates with people's struggles. Apt liturgy aims to open up the Bible to people and to showcase Jesus;

♦ A period of prayer. However, the *priest* may well code switch[14] and invite people to quietly reflect rather than, or in addition to, using the word 'prayer'. Within this time of prayer or quiet reflection, the priest will fashion words that acknowledge (name) private fears, sorrows and struggles, or what otherwise would be unarticulated distress;

♦ Putting people's deepest sadness and anxieties into a wider, universal context in order to emphasize that we are not alone in our struggle; it is shared by others either in the past or in other places;

♦ An acknowledgement that it may be comforting to trust that our God also shares our griefs and longs for our healing and health;

♦ Some kind of simple, symbolic act that holds together the struggle and hope that has been acknowledged during the liturgy.

A liturgy for neighbourhood renewal

The word 'liturgy' comes from a Greek word meaning 'work of the people'. Therefore, liturgy is appropriately taken into the wider community and offered as a public event. In areas of multiple deprivation there is now an extraordinary opportunity to offer the essentially public work of liturgy. Government policy, informed by concern about the eroded levels of trust and evaporating social capital, seeks to involve local people in identifying the priorities for their neighbourhood and in shaping public services in response to these priorities (see Chapter 3 for a more detailed exposition of this). The regeneration, or renewal, that the government seeks relates to the environment, the public services and even the renewal of hope in the hearts and minds of the people. In order to emphasize the depth of change the government uses words and concepts that have a Christian root. Furthermore, churches and other faith communities are invited to play an active part in the process of neighbourhood renewal. It is through this involvement in neighbourhood forums that the opportunity for apt liturgy arises, because apt liturgy is essentially about hope amidst struggles as is neighbourhood renewal.

The process of neighbourhood renewal or regeneration is often characterized by false starts, disappointments, resentments, misunderstandings and disputes. It is a fraught process especially in the early stages as different groups and individuals jockey for position. Trust, rather than being built up, can easily be destroyed. And rather than hope being generated, a deeper cynicism can develop, leading to repeated crises and disputes. Because of this there will very likely be a need to mark a fresh start and renewed willingness to trust neighbours and the agencies working in the neighbourhood.[15] The availability of apt liturgy can provide an opportunity for all involved to experience the power of apology, to acknowledge what is good and what needs to be cherished and provide an opportunity to admit the need to change for the better as people, as neighbours and as a community.

Russ Parker's emphasis on healing, and particularly healing wounded history, is very relevant to the construction of such a liturgy. Each neighbourhood has its own distinctive story. Some parts of the story will be edifying, other aspects might be shameful or indicate repeated disappointments. Acknowledging past grievances and distress is not just about preparing the ground in readiness for a fresh start. It is much more than this. By revisiting and taking seriously the explicit and hidden messages from local history we lessen the likelihood of dysfunctional history repeating itself in that place. No one can build a firm, new life through hatred of the past. Apt liturgy has the capacity to acknowledge these past dynamics, and to do so with lightness of touch and sensitivity, harnessing a matter-of-fact manner that does not drift into blaming and reopening past wounds. The prayers and reflections that form part of the apt liturgy can embrace the depth of the story that claims and entraps the neighbourhood.

In preparing for this public liturgy it is important to invite people of faith (and maybe people of different faiths) within the neighbourhood to pray for the event as well as to encourage their involvement. Preparatory work needs to be done with those people who are most involved in the stuck situation, seeking their acknowledgement of the need for a fresh start, and the part that the power of apology can play in this. This is the toughest part of the groundwork along with living with the sniggers from those who think the idea of apt liturgy is a silly idea. In introducing the idea of the liturgy to people and seeking their cooperation it may be helpful to use the example of Yom Kippur. This Jewish festival is known by name by many outside the Jewish community but people may not be familiar with its significance: asking each other and God to set us free from the effects of our dismay. The apt liturgy for a regeneration or renewal project wanting to have a fresh start is akin to this Jewish liturgy in seeking to free a community from cynicism and disappointment.[16]

At the outset, or *the gathering*, the liturgy might incorporate some of the following sentences:

> As we gather in this place we meet each other as neighbours, as friends, as people who work in this community. We meet as people who want the best for this community and yet we come together aware of the struggles and limitations that affect us.

> We meet with the shared intention of working together for a positive future for our neighbourhood. We meet also with the awareness that shared life cannot thrive without give and take. We come with a willingness to let go of hurts and offer forgiveness and receive forgiveness from each other.

> In meeting together in this way we renew the possibility of friendship and a shared commitment to the well-being of our

community. As we meet together today we recognize that we need to hear not just facts and opinions but the pain that is in each other's hearts.

We will seek grace to be set free from the resentment that each of us carries. We will seek grace to be free from the power of frustration and anger.

We will acknowledge the pain of broken relationships, not just in this place, but in other places in the world.

Russ Parker[17] identifies five stages in relation to the process of healing wounded history and this provides a helpful structure for many expressions of apt liturgy, and in particular for a liturgy which aims to prompt a fresh start in relation to neighbourhood renewal and other regeneration programmes. The first of the five stages he identifies is *remembering*. This means that the liturgy needs to give room for the telling of the specific story around which the apt liturgy is focused. The person leading the liturgy may provide a summary, or representative people may do this.[18] In the context of a community trying to pull together in response to regeneration and neighbourhood renewal initiatives it may be possible for people to be given the opportunity to speak of their biggest grief or disappointment associated with the process.

One of the essential features of apt liturgy is putting alongside the local story a story from Scripture, ideally a story that involves Jesus. In the context of neighbourhood renewal it may be relevant to draw on readings from Nehemiah and the challenge of rebuilding Jerusalem (see Nehemiah 4); Micah, whose message alternates between oracles of doom and oracles of hope; Matthew 21, the parable of the tenants; Mark 12.41–44, the importance of the widow's contribution; or John 1.46, where the question is posed, 'Can anything good come out of Nazareth?' might also be considered. The reading from Scripture can be supported with a homily. It may be appropriate for the story of people's disappointment and dismay to be incorporated within the homily.

The second stage that Parker identifies is *lamenting*, the sense of having one's griefs heard. In the liturgy this could mean inviting people to light a candle for each of the disappointments and disturbances that they have experienced in relation to the regeneration or renewal programme, possibly with people lighting a candle and naming very briefly other people's concerns and griefs. However, people need to be protected from feeling under pressure to do this, so that they can also feel able to light a candle and *in silence* acknowledge other people's griefs and concerns.

The third stage that Parker identifies is *confessing*. This means owning that we have *all* done wrong. This might take the form of the following:

> Let us begin by recognizing that to mess up, and to be less than helpful and less than straightforward is something that we all do. So we own before each other that we accept our faults and mistakes and have no wish to cover them up.
>
> And we seek grace to free ourselves from thinking 'How could they do such a thing?'
>
> We offer to each other our willingness to work on each other's behalf.

The fourth stage that Parker identifies is *repentance*. This is about a commitment to a new way. The liturgy could take the form of a commitment.

> We commit ourselves:
>   To seek freedom from the rush for power;
>   To seek freedom from ignoring the dignity and rights of others;
>   To seek freedom from demonizing others;
>   To seek freedom from making people dependent on me;
>   To seek freedom from fudging issues, rather than speaking plainly and honestly.

The fifth and final stage that Parker identifies is *forgiveness*. This is about letting go of the grievances that we hold against each other:

We acknowledge our shared fellowship of inadequacy and ask each other to be generous with forgiveness.
Together we choose forgiveness rather than harbouring resentment.
We seek to create a future that is not bound by the destructiveness of the past.
We reach out to a time when we can rejoice in shared commitment and shared achievement on behalf of our community.
We wish for us all, and for this place, a new life and a new hope. We seek renewal of our hearts and energy, and a commitment to work together and to share a vision for the flourishing of this place.

Before concluding the liturgy it may be appropriate to give some time to naming those places in the world where people also need to find the way of forgiving each other for past wrongs. People could even be invited to 'buzz' in groups of two or three to work together to name the place for which they have a particular concern. The liturgy would then conclude with a vision not just of the flourishing of this neighbourhood but of the world itself.

In conclusion of the liturgy it may be feasible to push the church doors wide open or open the doors of the community centre into another room where there can be a celebration, with people able to share informally and begin to practise their new beginning.

Apt liturgy: some wider issues

The aim of such liturgy is to help people to move from struggle and dismay, towards hope and re-engagement with life. The ability to achieve this belongs distinctly to the Church. However, apt liturgy in the context of the foundational domain is sub-Christian, but its purpose is to move people in the direction of the explicit presentation of the Gospel. To create openness to the Gospel there are emphases that are particularly important to incorporate within apt liturgy:

Reconciliation

The divine commission that Christians and the Church have received is to be channels of reconciliation, i.e. to encourage processes that bring together those who are estranged. Familiarity with the idea of reconciliation is essential if a foundation is to be provided for the explicit presentation of the good news of our reconciliation with God through Jesus.

Grace

It may be necessary within the liturgy to explain what grace means, for grace is a little known word. However, intuitively, people sense its embracing and reassuring nature. Grace means to be given more than we deserve. Grace is about knowing what it is to be given a break, and to be treated better than we deserve. The capacity to understand and be familiar with the idea of grace is essential if a foundation is to be provided for the explicit domain.

Solidarity

By encouraging people to link their specific struggles with more universal struggles solidarity is created. This may be a shared experience of loss or bereavement, of injustice or of the experience of resentment. By helping people to link their personal struggle with the struggles of those more distant encourages solidarity with those who would otherwise be dismissed as strangers. The recognition of fraternal relations is essential if we are to begin to appreciate that we are all children of the same heavenly Father. Furthermore, this process sets in train a number of important dynamics essential to the idea of holistic mission, for it represents a movement towards God's Kingdom and an awakening to the salvation of God.

Helping people to link their specific distress with the distress experienced by those in distant places also primes people in relation to a greater awareness of the prevalence of sin. So, for example, the resentment that generates a host of negativities on a housing estate is the same emotion that generates racial hatred and murderous intent. The same destructive cycle links the housing estate with the slaughter of neighbours in Rwanda.

Most likely apt liturgy[19] has to embrace tough and distressing emotions and provide people with some spiritual shelter. It provides the words, constructs and symbols that can inform and encourage people's intuitive awareness of God and, because of its precision in coming alongside people in their distress, can greatly enhance a person's spiritual development, to the extent of triggering a religious experience. The capacity of apt liturgy to provoke or trigger a religious experience, or at least to move people to tears, is important to the task of rehabilitating the business of Church and formal religion in people's eyes. Apt liturgy, provided by the Church, can demonstrate that formal religion and the local church are an effective vehicle for spirituality.

Religious experience and the growth of a moral sensitivity

The foundational domain is enlivened by religious experiences, meaningful patterns of events and superstitions. From the perspective of the institutional Church this is a pretty chaotic sphere but it is a very powerful one because of its capacity to deepen people's sense of God's nearness and involvement in their lives. David Hay's work[20] suggests that the majority of adults in Britain will have had an experience that is 'not everyday' and in which they felt the involvement of a 'presence or power' in their lives.

There is a pattern associated with the occurrence of religious experience. Often a religious experience is triggered by a time of stress, perhaps associated with sudden illness or some kind of personal crisis. I remember I had a very clear example of this in an interview I conducted whilst working as a researcher with the Religious Experience Research Unit. I interviewed a man in his later years. He spoke very straight-forwardly about an experience he had had in hospital. He was about to undergo major surgery. In the interview he said 'The ward sister said to me, "Don't worry, God is looking after you." And I felt that. I was relying on God and religion, I'm a human being.'[21] This experience, despite its simplicity illustrates three important issues:

◆ personal crises open us up to an awareness of God's alongsideness;
◆ reaching out to God in a time of crisis is to act like a human being;
◆ to communicate that God is concerned with our distress (as the ward sister did)[22] can be profoundly reassuring and of immense practical value.

On the basis of David Hay's work we can conclude that the majority of people, of all ages, will have had a personal experience of God's presence in their lives.[23] The research is now so robust that the persistence of religious experience, despite secular pressures, suggests that we have a biological capacity for such perceptions. The root of this biological capacity being the fact that religious experience has survival value for the species and it is for this reason that it has persisted. This is good news for the work we need to do in relation to the foundational domain. However, it highlights the fact that the task is not so much one of trying to infuse people with an awareness of God, but rather of helping people to explore the implications of such an experience.

Traditionally the Church has discouraged, or even dismissed, religious experience. It has fostered the view that it is only the rare saint who experiences God's intimate involvement in his or her life. Ordinary people were discouraged from talking about[24] and having confidence in their religious experience because the potency and authority carried by a religious experience could easily trump what is on offer from the Church. In the days when the Church prized its authority to supervise and shape the way people thought, religious experience was viewed as a disruptive force which was hard to control. Religious experience is potentially subversive, for it undermines the claim by religious dignitaries that they provide the channel by which to encounter God.

Jurgen Moltmann, like David Bosch, encourages a wide view of salvation. He writes, 'Salvation does not mean merely salvation of the soul, individual rescue from the evil of the world, comfort to the troubled conscience, but also the realization of the eschatological hope of justice, the humanizing of man, the socializing of humanity, peace for all creation.'[25] In seeking to express and put into practice this fulsome view of salvation the Church has to take religious experience seriously because of its capacity to provoke an enhanced moral sense, as well as the awareness of God being alongside and accessible.

The foundational domain requires the Church to expect and respect the religious experiences that so many people cherish in their hearts, despite the fact that they may be unorthodox and zany. There is a second reason for this hospitality towards religious experience. It is because very often the person who has had a religious experience reports that as a result they have become more thoughtful and more moral[26] in their dealings with others. Increasingly it is being recognized that religious experience can bring about a greater awareness of, as well as a sympathetic response to, the needs of others. In particular, the research undertaken by Rebecca Nye in relation to children's spirituality has led her to contend that spirituality and, in particular, religious experience are of real benefit to the quality of communal relations and civic society. Nye has coined the term *relational consciousness* to describe this increased attentiveness to the well-being of others, and even to the world itself. Nye suggests that this enlightenment and alertness to the needs of others is a natural and universal dynamic[27] associated with religious experience. She writes that religious experience and the spirituality associated with it, lead to a 'Radical divestiture of posses-siveness, self-centredness and even of ordinary attachments to the results of actions. . . . Spirituality is the bedrock on which rests the welfare, not only of the individual, but also of society, and indeed the health of our entire planetary environment.'[28]

If it is the case that religious experience and an active spirituality sustain human community then this is profoundly important in the light of the haemorrhage of social capital and trust that has overcome our communities and our institutions. The question of how to remoralize our corporate life is baf-fling to most experts because it is clear that the restoration of trust cannot be achieved head-on. No one can order someone to trust; to require or even request someone to trust imme-diately arouses suspicion. Nor can people be requested to be friendly, warm and helpful to their neighbour. All this does is provoke suspicion and more distrust. Trust is one of those complex phenomena that can only be built up obliquely. Religious experience and the associated development of personal spirituality provide an oblique route by which to remoralize our relationships with each other and increase the desire for social justice.

Religious experience, like apt liturgy, is likely to be sub-Christian. The concepts and ideas that surround religious experience are likely to be rooted in folk religion rather than Christian orthodoxy. It is essential that this lack of orthodoxy is accepted rather than dismissed or shaped by the for-mularies of the institutionalized Church. For this reason hospitality to religious experience is an attribute of the foundational domain. Furthermore, religious experience is also significant to the vocational domain as will be shown in chapter 10.

Hospitality and autonomy in the foundational domain

Throughout the Bible there are many instances where hospitality is a central theme. Hospitality is one of the few themes that is referred to consistently in both the Old and New Testaments and its centrality is endorsed by the Early Church. Hospitality is a very precise concept and its radical nature should not be underestimated. Hospitality is one of those rare situations where the person most in control of the situation, the host, has all the obligations and the vulnerable or less powerful guest has almost all the rights.[29]

Hospitality is essential to the foundational domain, because when the Church works in the foundational domain is has to be hospitable to God of a thousand names and the chaotic perceptions of those who pick and mix their beliefs and preferences. However, this hospitality to people's varied ideas, beliefs and religious experiences has to involve more than dialogue and debate because hospitality calls for the host to be open to learning from the guest. Notably, in giving hospitality the host must not try to change the guest, and the host must grant the guest the right to remain a stranger, accepting the possibility of no personal exchange or significant encounter occurring between host and guest. The guest has the right to remain a mystery to his or her host, for that is how we come to entertain angels unawares.

Translating the principles of hospitality into the foundational domain means that the guest, or the 'other' has to be granted *autonomy*. This means accepting in the other what we do not understand or agree with, and allowing the other person's autonomy to be on a par with our own. This may jar with our inclination to press the person to at least examine the gift of salvation that is so close to hand. But hospitality requires us to control our proselytizing urges. When we work in the foundational domain we enable people to gather concepts and insights at their own pace. The hard reality is that to rush to a complete or systematic presentation of salvation through Jesus is risky. For example, at a time when child abuse receives such a high profile, to speak of Christ's death on the cross for our sake risks leaving the impression of a Father who is deranged, damaged and implacable. When working in the foundational domain it is as important to avoid giving people a reason to reject the tenets of our faith as it is to share those tenets.

The work that we do in the foundational domain grants people autonomy to reflect in their own way and is respectful of their unbelief. Fostering the habit of respectfulness not only equips us to do business in the post-modern world; it can also generate some unexpected and positive outcomes:

♦ *The acknowledgement that others' autonomy and capacity for truth-seeking strengthen the self*

This psychological insight is relevant to the Church and to Christians. We have taken such a pasting over the last century that we would not be human if our self-confidence had not been dented. Whilst self-confidence is not usually cited as one of the Christian virtues the absence of self-confidence (or the presence of the opposite – timidity or insecurity) makes for a far from healthy group or individual. A person or group lacking in self-confidence is unlikely to grant respect for others. It follows, therefore, that the insecure are unlikely to be at ease with the foundational domain where hospitality to those who have different or no beliefs is essential. Likewise, it could be argued that the ability to invest in the hospitality and respectfulness that are essential to the foundational domain is a sign that health is returning to the Church.

♦ *The offering of a hospitable free space may allow change to come about*

If we take the potency of grace seriously then hospitality will have a transforming impact. However, we cannot offer hospitality and maintain the expectation of transformation for to do so destroys hospitality. However, as with other complex and potent dynamics, the principle of obliquity has to be heeded. Hospitality has to be offered generously and with an open hand if it is to carry the possibility of transformation. If the potential for transformation is addressed head-on hospitality loses this capacity, in fact it ceases to be hospitality.

♦ *Solidarity in sinfulness is discovered*

Hospitality involves tolerance because it requires accepting in the other what we may not understand or agree with. The danger with this degree of tolerance is that it requires the suspension of judgement, and this is naive given our sinfulness. There are some things to which we should not be hospitable. The difficulty we have is that our history has demonstrated that our perception of what and who are sinful is invariably contaminated by hegemonic smog. Rather than ignore sin, the way through is to embrace the fact that we all have fallen short, we are all sinners. By owning deeply our vulnerability to error we can embrace the deep humility that results. It is only with this frame of mind that we have open hands. By acknowledging our part in the struggle of sinfulness we can genuinely offer apt liturgy and invite people to join with us in acknowledging how prone we *all* are to being overwhelmed by struggles that seem too hard to bear.

Just as the *raison d'être* of a business is to make a profit from the product it sells, the *raison d'être* of the Church is to articulate an enduring hope that comes because Jesus has conquered sin. However, if the customer or market has no awareness of sinfulness then there is no call for the product. The foundational domain and the associated hospitality is where we help people acknowledge their state of sin. However, it is not a place of condemnation, it is a place of solidarity. For sin is a fact of our corporate and personal lives, no one is excluded from it or by it. When we acknowledge that we are stuck and that hope has failed us, we begin to recognize our need for a saviour – and at this point people have moved into the explicit domain.

The image from the Gospels of hospitality that affirms these positives is the Great Banquet. The king, having been let down by the original guests goes out to the highways and byways and makes a party out of the most unlikely. In Luke 14 nothing is expected of these unlikely guests other than that they accept the invitation. However, the version in Matthew 22 concludes with a far more challenging coda. Here, the king's hospitality is withdrawn when he sees a guest dressed inappropriately; and the guest is not just thrown out of the banquet, he is hurled into a place where there is much wailing and gnashing of teeth. These two versions of the same story epitomize the tension at the heart of hospitality. In being hospitable do we have to put up with anything? Does hospitality require us to suspend judgement and tolerate anything and everything? Is there no place for challenge in relation to hospitality? Can the host never make demands on the guest?

The answer is that the host has to trust that God, through the Holy Spirit, will make demands on the guest. The evidence regarding the prevalence of religious experience should give us reassurance that God will draw alongside and, because of our hospitality, the person may feel able to name that reassuring, hope-filled presence in their lives as God – a heavenly, caring God who offers the intimacy of the eternal. In maintaining the discipline of open-handed hospitality we should be encouraged by Gerard Hughes' observation that we need to 'Walk gently because God has walked there before'.[30] Furthermore, when God draws close to our guests, not only is hope aroused, so too is a new morality. The guest becomes aware of the part they play in cherishing and building up others and the creation itself.

Summary

The foundational domain is a new field for evangelism that has come into being because of the ending of a Christendom culture. Our evangelistic strategies have to take account of the loss of the Christian narrative as a dominant world view. The foundational domain is where evangelists work to:

♦ encourage people to take seriously the *possibility* of God
♦ acknowledge our solidarity in sinfulness;
♦ offer concepts and symbols that help people become more competent in relation to spiritual matters.

Work in the foundational domain is not for those with puny faith or feeble self-confidence. Rather it calls for patience, acceptance and generosity of spirit if the essential hospitality of the foundational domain is to be maintained.

It is important that our work in the foundational domain serves the explicit domain. The foundational domain helps people to establish the possibility of God existing 'out there', thus providing a foundation to enable a movement from God 'out there' to God that exists in people's hearts and minds. By fostering a process of recognition, i.e. helping people to recognize the action of God in their lives and the relevance of God to their lives, people are more likely to understand the Gospel when it is expounded and interpreted in the explicit domain. The explicit domain is where the message of salvation and the practice of hope are expressed.

The explicit domain has over the centuries gathered a plethora of secondary activities and associations. The Gospel does not need these accretions. The resource problem that we face because of maintaining the accretions associated with the explicit domain leaves little spare for the foundational domain. However, until the tasks that belong to the foundational domain can be defined and the skills that need to accompany them are identified, it is difficult to make a case that resources should be diverted from the explicit domain. This chapter is an attempt to contribute to this process.

The tasks and roles that have been identified as most relevant to the foundational domain are:

♦ the role of chaplain, whether to a football club, a university or a hospice;

♦ the ability to provide apt liturgy especially where people are losing hope;
♦ heeding the discipline of hospitality especially in relation to religious experience.

There is a fourth task which is important to foundational domain and that is to open up our churches and other buildings for use by the wider community. This is such an important aspect of hospitality, and in recent years has received the most significant investment of resources, that it needs to be considered in a chapter of its own.

Notes

1 John O'Donohue, 'Minding the Threshold – Towards a Theory of Priesthood in Difficult Times' in *The Furrow*, 49(6): 323–35; June 1998, p. 325.
2 This is an example of symbolic interactionism. The intense media coverage of legal action against a number of priests who in the past have been guilty of child abuse has served to associate in people's mind the symbol of priest with child abuse. The potency of the media in shaping our symbolic perceptions is both rapid and virtually comprehensive. As yet we have yet to discover a method by which reputation can be restored once the media have destroyed the trust in an institution.
3 John O'Donohue, op. cit., pp. 329 and 332.
4 Hospital chaplaincy in particular has a low threshold that is essential to the foundational domain. In hospital it is now a requirement that communion is received by *intinction*, i.e. the wafer is dipped into the wine rather than people drinking from the same cup. However much this development might be abhorred by those committed to the orthodoxy of the explicit domain it represents the lowering of an important psychological barrier represented by the perceived lack of hygiene associated with 40 or so people drinking from the same cup.

5 Kids, and adults as well, are now frequently lost in other worlds – the other worlds offered by computer games. For the most part these games are what are known as 3D shooters, in which a heavily armed hero takes on the world in a range of scenarios, shooting his or, in the case of Lara Croft, her way out of trouble when assailed by more and more 'bots'. However, a growing number of games are RPGs – Role Playing Games, often assigning the player to the role of 'God', a tycoon or city mayor. Whether this habit of role playing, supported by a Play-Station, aids the imagination or inhibits it requires a more informed assessment than I can offer.

6 The rapidity with which tastes now change makes it quite possible that in time church music and church ambience will become highly prized. The signifier of this will be when *The Rough Guide to London* recommends Evensong at Westminster Abbey as the best free chill in the capital!

7 See for example, Robin Gill, *Churchgoing and Christian Ethics* (Cambridge: Cambridge University Press, 1991), pp. 132–3; and in particular, Philip Richter and Leslie J. Francis, *Gone But Not Forgotten: Church Leaving and Returning* (London: Darton, Longman and Todd, 1988); The Church Army's 'Sheffield Centre' under its director George Lings is also a source of research on this distinction.

8 In the 2001 census, a surprising 71 per cent described themselves as Christian. It would seem that God gets a thumbs up whilst the steady decline in church involvement suggests that involvement in organized religion continues to get a thumbs down.

9 In my book *Beyond the Good Samaritan* I coined the term 'apt liturgy' to describe the occasions when I had been part of a special liturgy that had been designed to focus on or highlight a specific, community-ministry initiative. I was surprised by the amount of interest the concept generated and the speed with which the term

'apt liturgy' has been adopted. I have since reflected on the idea more thoroughly and endeavour to share my reflections in this section.

10 The apt liturgy took place on the return of the minibus from the day trip. Instead of just dropping people off at the entrance to their flats it went firstly to the Manse. A sensitive minister would be aware that time was at a premium because people would be needing to 'spend a penny'!

11 I use the word priest deliberately. However, I do so with an acknowledgement of the priesthood of all believers. I use the word priest in this context because it best describes the role that is being undertaken. For in apt liturgy the role of the priest is to mediate or give expression to God's involvement in or alongsideness in relation to the struggle.

12 This business of candles provides a wonderful example of symbolic interactionism. Whilst those schooled in different expressions of churchmanship might be willing to fight to the death about the rights and wrongs of candles, for the unschooled, a candle is a symbol for personal hopes and struggle, and carries an intimation of eternity. In a context where low, earthbound symbols dominate we should be grateful that in this symbolic darkness people still feel able to light a candle.

13 John O'Donohue, op. cit., p. 332.

14 I borrow the term *code switch* from Basil Bernstein. Bernstein studied the linguistic codes used by different social classes. He noted the capacity of children to *code switch* (between a restricted and an elaborated code) according to their situation. A similar capacity is required if we are to work successfully in the foundational domain. See Basil Bernstein, *Theoretical Studies Towards a Sociology of Language*, Vol. 1 (London: Routledge and Kegan Paul, 1977).

15 Too often the fresh start in regeneration programmes is achieved by the chief officer of the programme being

sacked or resigning. There is something quite distressing at the speed with which the optimism of regeneration and renewal proposals disintegrates and can spread negativity rather than build people up.

16 There is a great incentive to sort out disputes in relation to neighbourhood renewal and in New Deal for Community programmes: unless the community is 'together' and leaders in agreement, the Government Office in the region will not authorize the release of monies.

17 Ibid., p. 81.

18 In the context of apt liturgy this telling of the story can be far more concise than would be the case in the process that Parker commends in relation to healing wounded history. The aim of apt liturgy is not to elicit hidden emotions that need to surface before healing is possible. Apt liturgy is about handling *hard, obvious* emotions. Its aim is to allow the possibility of hope to percolate the dismay that has enveloped people.

19 There are instances where apt liturgy can be celebratory, e.g. the blessing of a community playground or a liturgy of blessing for a group going on an adventure.

20 David Hay, *Religious Experience Today: Studying The Facts* (London: Cassell/Mowbray, 1990).

21 This experience is referred to in the paper 'Secular Society? Religious Meanings: A Contemporary Paradox' (1985) by David Hay and Ann Morisy, *Review of Religious Research* **26**(3): 213–27.

22 I have spoken with nurses about this man's experience, and they comment that to act as the ward sister had done would no longer be considered acceptable behaviour. One might argue that offering such reassurance is the role of the hospital chaplain. However, intuitively, one suspects the ward sister's comment would have greater impact than the hospital chaplain – because of the principle of obliquity. After all, the hospital chaplain is paid to utter such reassurances.

23 In the light of this high prevalence of positive and

'immediate' sense of God, those of us who are fond of the institutional Church have to face up to some searching questions. What is the basis of this gap between people's sense of the presence of God and the prevailing view of the woefulness of organized religion? And more importantly, how do we organize ourselves to ensure that the relevance of the Gospel of Jesus is shared with people who already know the reality of God? For this reason alone the Church must give maximum priority to the foundational domain.

24 My own research into religious experience suggests that a quarter of those who could report a religious experience had never spoken of the experience prior to them being interviewed. See Ann Morisy 'The Problems of a Sociological Definition of Religious Experience' (1986) University of Nottingham, unpublished M. Phil.

25 Jurgen Moltmann, *The Theology of Hope* (London: SCM, 1983), p. 329.

26 *Moral* meaning the actions of people towards each other and in relation to the wider world.

27 David Hay with Rebecca Nye, *'The Spirit of the Child'* (London, Harper Collins, 1998), p. 144

28 Ibid., p. 153.

29 Harry Murray provides a thorough outline of the traditional Christian and cultural understanding of hospitality. See Chapter One 'Hospitality as Social Relationship' in his book *Do Not Neglect Hospitality* (Philadelphia: Temple University Press, 1990).

30 Quoted by Melvyn Matthews (ed.) in *Finding Your Own Story* (London: Darton, Longman and Todd, 1992). p. 62.

9

Church Community Centres and the Foundational Domain

The insights associated with hospitality can usefully inform one of the most significant aspects of the foundational domain in which the Church has so far invested: the development of seven day a week church-community centres. There is a sturdy history of churches being used flexibly. However our Victorian forebears judged that it was disrespectful to use churches for anything but worship, and so they filled them with pews to ensure that nothing inappropriate could take place. Today churches are increasingly shaking off this demarcation. Up and down the country congregations have made a great effort to adapt large Victorian churches for flexible use – worship on Sundays and community use throughout the week.

The availability of churches and church halls for use by the wider community is one of the taken-for-granted aspects of British life. Community groups of all kinds, formal groups, spontaneous groups, weddings and birthday parties have all found space in the church hall down the road. This easy availability of church halls and church centres is one of the underestimated contributions by churches to social capital and social cohesion in many local communities. Churches have proved more successful than local authorities and tenants and residents' groups at running and maintaining facilities for community groups.[1] However, what churches have been less successful at is tracking and articulating how this open, and often generous access, translates into mission.

I can already hear people protesting that the use of church facilities by the wider community must not be reduced to a narrow, instrumental outcome that serves the Church's interests. I agree. The demands of hospitality require an open-handed and unconditional welcome to (almost) all comers.[2] However, there is a caution that needs to be put alongside this generosity of spirit. What if people using the church/community centre, as well as the passers-by, don't catch hold of the idea of the church being hospitable or generous? This possibility comes into better focus with the insights associated with symbolic interactionism.

> I think of one church that spent four years fund-raising and renovating their massive church building both inside and out. A number of voluntary organizations became 'tenants' and everything seemed to have worked to plan. Except that no one who passed by or entered the building on a weekday had any idea that this was 'church' in a new and relevant mode. This was despite the fact that the wrought-iron railings outside the church had been repaired and repainted and the church noticeboard neatly presented the services in tasteful maroon with gold lettering. All this traditional representation of 'church' was trumped by the large, brightly coloured PVC banners that had been bought for £40 a piece and had been hung on the smartly painted railings to advertise the services offered by each of the voluntary organizations. The message that came over was that this was once a church and now it is a community centre.

Whilst the leadership of the church may feel that the new facilities provide a new and lower threshold that encourages the wider community to encounter the church, for those outside the church the mundane symbols associated with a community building can easily dominate their perceptions. The vast majority of people who are not involved in church life will probably look upon the newly created church centre within the church building as indicative of it retreating from its former capacity. They may perceive the new facilities as being about generating income by a church strapped for cash, or even the church handing over its premises to some other initiative run by the neighbourhood forum or local authority. Rather than communicating relevance and hospitality, the community facilities can easily communicate that the church has given up and quit the scene. Skill at 'impression management' and minimizing 'unmeant gestures'[3] are essential if churches are to avoid confirming people's suspicions that churches are in terminable decline.

We need to take seriously the possibility that rather than being perceived as a new way of being church and an extension of ministry and mission, opening up our churches for community use can feed into the dominant view that churches are failing. It is possible to counteract this view – if only we think to do it with boldness and imagination. This means briefing the architect to ensure that the high symbols of the Church and symbols that speak of some thing 'other' need to permeate the everyday, community areas. Ideally the architect will find a way of using the full space of the church without requiring expensively built partitions which define one area for the community and the other for the church. An open-plan church will probably provide as much flexibility and scope for a number of activities at the same time (including lighting a candle and saying a prayer), as can be achieved in a demarcated community centre built within the church.

It is essential that some way is found to transmit the message that the Church is still active and healthily involved in the adapted building. This must involve ensuring that the signs and noticeboards, both inside and out, are 'customized' and carry some kind of signature that speaks of the Church. The explicit information on a notice or sign is only one aspect of its impact. There will be an implicit message as well. The implicit message has to be one that says that the Church is holding the space so that others can find their place. Transmitting an appropriate, implicit message takes an expert. This means it must be included in the budget for fitting out the renovated building. It also means that regular users of the building need to be willing to cooperate, both at the outset and in the long term. This has to be reflected in the lease or hiring agreements, indicating the right of the church to provide signage throughout the building, and the need for approval for any other signage that lessees would like.

A related but significant issue that churches have to address is the use of the word 'services'. Again it is a matter of symbolic interactionism. Most organizations when they talk about 'services' mean the 'products' or 'outcomes' that they can provide for people. So, on the multicoloured banners that bedecked the newly painted railings surrounding the newly renovated church, one of the voluntary organizations advertised its services:

♦ Skilled and friendly instructors
♦ A place specially adapted for people with disabilities
♦ A more healthy life – at no cost to you
♦ Call in now for a warm welcome

The church, in gold lettering, also advertised its services:

Sunday Service 10.00 a.m.
Holy Communion and Sunday School
Marriages and Baptisms
by appointment with the Vicar   tel . . .

The impact might not be that of the church having quit, but of a church in a time warp. If we are to take seriously the tasks associated with the foundational domain we have to revisit the idea of *services* being what churches do. The services that the church offers need to be expressed in terms of the foundational rather than the explicit domain. In developing an integrated approach to weekday as well as Sunday use of church buildings the church should not see its role as providing services (in the sense of worship) but as recognizing and promoting the other humanizing outcomes that 'Church' generates. Rather than focusing on what we do (i.e. worship and fellowship groups), we need to articulate the likely outcomes of our work. If we were to use the word 'services' in the same way as the wider community we could fill our own share of multicoloured banners, proclaiming:

Find what works for you...
♦ Explore wide perspectives on life and its challenges
♦ Values for your children
♦ Get involved in issues of concern
♦ Join a truly diverse, accepting community
Call in now for a warm welcome

The hospitality that is so essential to the foundational domain calls for commitment to a generalized good will and vision of inclusive, human flourishing. We could proclaim a lot more but that would be to trespass into the explicit domain and sacrifice the message of inclusivity, which is vital to the foundational domain, and the need to improve social cohesion in so many neighbourhoods.

A holistic view of mission calls for a commitment to build 'Godly human community'[4] as much as it calls for helping people to do business with God. However, to do this requires a far more proactive approach than just providing premises for community use. If the church committed to community involvement is to move people from the foundational domain towards the explicit domain where the deep message of hope through Jesus can be communicated, it too has to adopt a purposeful strategy. As more and more churches make their building available to the wider community there is a pressing need for a new role, or to use ecclesiastical jargon, we need a new ministry. I suggest we call this role *community chaplain*.

Community chaplain(s) and church centres

The role of community chaplain can be undertaken by trained volunteers. It may be that a church has two or three community chaplains, just as happens with readers or lay preachers. The most obvious task of a community chaplain would be to call in regularly to the groups using the church centre or hall. However, the role has four aims:

♦ to encourage people to 'do business with God';
♦ to bring greater integration of Sunday church life with the weekday activities;
♦ to present the church centre as a new way of being church rather than the church rationalizing its resources or wanting to generate income;
♦ to build a sense of corporate identity across centre users (and congregation) in a manner that builds up social capital within the neighbourhood.

This role is essentially about being *priest for the everyday*, i.e. representing and, occasionally, speaking of God's alongside-ness in relation to daily life, whether the moment is filled with delight, stress or struggle. The role of community chaplain is a practical expression of the *priesthood of all believers*. However, there are important boundary issues that have to be addressed if such a role is to be viable. It is important that the role does not drift into pastoral care as the role of community chaplain is primarily about ministering to groups rather than individuals. Unless this boundary is maintained the role will drift into that of pastor or that of the traditional model of priest. It is also important that those who hire the premises are alerted to the likelihood of occasional visits by a community chaplain, and that they accept this.[5]

In order to distinguish a community chaplain from a curate or minister it may be helpful to list the tasks and responsibilities that a community chaplain might undertake:

1. Getting a routine of calling in on regular and occasional users of the church centre, with a view to providing prayer support and attentive listening.
2. Being alert to pastoral issues arising from the users of the centre *and to make appropriate referrals*.

3. To host events to which all associated with the centre and church are invited. These events to should characterized by fun and laughter.

4. Being alert to issues/opportunities in the community that may be relevant to those using the facilities and support the groups in their involvement in these issues and initiatives.

5. Being alert to opportunities for *apt liturgy* and involve others in this.

6. Building links between the Sunday congregation and the weekday 'congregations' both in terms of communication and activities (in the wider world this is called networking!).

7. Hosting weekday events, which encourage reflection, linking everyday life and matters of faith, inviting both Sunday and weekday users of the facilities.

As with other 'ministries' there needs to be specific training for those willing to take on the role.[6] The role helps the Church to have the prowess and alertness to know when to act with courage, such as it might in offering apt liturgy, taking action against loan sharks preying on the community, or protesting at the inadequate provision of home care for frail, elderly people. Added to this alertness to issues in the community is the skill of recognizing and handling anxiety. This too has to be part of the repertoire of skills of the community chaplain, and others who espouse community involvement and community development.

Taking account of anxiety

Anxiety affects everyone. All of us are inclined to organize our lives in ways that lessen our anxiety levels. Anxiety does dastardly things to us when it becomes acute, or worse still, when it is chronic or long term. Anxiety levels rise as the level of trust falls, anxiety levels and the level of social capital in a community are in inverse relationship. This means that in poor communities where trust between neighbours has eroded or trust between the community and the service providers (e.g. schools, housing officers, police, etc.) has broken down anxiety will increase. In some situations this may have become a long-term or chronic state.

Heightened anxiety makes us react rather than respond. Although there is only a split-second difference between responding and reacting, there is a huge difference in the outcome. When we react we become more instinctual, and our behaviour is likely to be extreme and unyielding. In fact, research into brain activity indicates that when we are anxious the most primitive part of the brain, the reptilian brain in the frontal lobe, shows increased activity. This extraordinary fact of our biological make-up says it all. When we are acutely anxious or long-term anxious we are more likely to act in a cold-blooded, unfeeling way.

The disturbing feature of anxiety is that it inclines people to scapegoat, i.e. to put the blame on someone – or some group. But there is more to it than this. With anxiety comes the inclination to pick on or expose those who are different. So in chronically anxious communities it will be asylum seekers who get blamed for the neighbourhood going to the dogs. It will be the homosexual couple who get their windows smashed because rumour has gone round that a paedophile has come to live on the estate. Unrecognized and uncontrolled anxiety exposes and makes vulnerable what is not alike.

When anxiety heightens most of us respond in a habitual way, and often we have learned these habits from our family of origin. For example, when we are anxious we are inclined to seek out others who will share our perceptions, i.e. to herd with others prepared to take on our hurts, or we will look for others with whom we gain a cheap solidarity by taking on their hurts and indignation – or fury. The other habitual way of responding to anxiety, especially when the anxiety is generated by conflict, is to distance ourselves from the person or situation that is perceived as being responsible for the conflict. By distancing ourselves we ensure that the situation can never be resolved, and worse still, by continually revisiting the unresolved pain cause the wound to fester rather than heal. Tragically for human relationships, herding and distancing are not mutually exclusive. It is quite possible for distancing to then generate herding, and before long the situation degenerates into hating.

Chronic or acute anxiety has other surprising repercussions. High anxiety often equates to low resilience. Those who minister in poor communities where anxiety levels are high may have intuitively recognized this. In particular it has an impact on the task of encouraging indigenous or local leadership. When anxious people are put in positions of leadership they are likely to become more anxious, and therefore less resilient. But more than this, when we are anxious we forget how to have fun. This fact alone makes for an unattractive individual or group. Only the most contrary of people are likely to join an acutely or chronically anxious group and this gives energy to a downward spiral as anxiety feeds decline and decline feeds anxiety.

This downward, even vicious cycle needs to heeded by those who make policies in the Church or in relation to regeneration programmes. The careless talk of an archdeacon, in issuing a threat that unless the roof is repaired the church will close, triggers an unholy process: preoccupation with worry dominates, self-absorption and fear shrinks people and, before long, chronic anxiety has set in. Resilience evaporates, people cease to enjoy each other's company and who would ever join such an unattractive group? Bingo, a full house of disasters is achieved. The New Deal Director issues a threat that money will not be released unless the Board and the Community Forum come to an agreement about priorities triggers an unholy process: the two groups distance themselves from each other rather than talk; blame starts to be allocated; people herd in agreement; and the two groups become more and more hostile to each other. Bingo, another full house.

A community chaplain can help dispel anxiety. In fact this

should be part of the role of anyone who works with communities and groups. This is not such a tall order. There are precise and particular steps that can be taken to lessen anxiety, and they are essential to the community practitioner's tool box. Essentially it involves working as a 'step down' transformer. Just as the transformer in a kid's train set reduces the voltage of the current so that kids and their dads are less likely to get electrocuted, likewise with anxiety, the skilled practitioner has the ability to reduce the voltage of the emotion that is in the system. One of the most important ways of doing this is to model or demonstrate ways of containing one's own anxiety. This capacity should not be confused with being 'laid back', although being able to resist being provoked is certainly an asset in anxiety-prone contexts.

There are four habits to cultivate and develop in others in the art of anxiety reduction:

1. To become aware of one's own reactive buttons. These are (metaphorical) buttons that people can press inadvertently and repeatedly and put us on edge. Most likely they have their root in our family or community of origin. My roots mean I have to work very hard to cope with authority figures. Somewhere in my past I have picked up an indelible message that authority figures are to be challenged. It is tempting to label such a pairing of reactive buttons as the components of an inferiority complex, but underneath such a label runs the deep river of anxiety. Each of us will have our own constellation of reactive buttons that continually trigger unwarranted reactions. Being aware of our own idiosyncratic buttons earns us that split-second grace that allows reaction to become a response.

2. To discipline both our heads and hearts that problems have multiple and interrelated causes. This 'systems approach' is essential if we are to prevent ourselves from falling prey to scapegoating.

3. A determination to resist picking up other people's anxieties. This requires a distinction to be made between listening and hearing people's gripes but not siding with them and getting caught up in the process of herding. The aim, rather, is to encourage people to take responsibility for their own feelings. When your ear is bent by someone who tells of a substantial litany of offences which have been committed against them, the response might be, 'What do you think *you* need to do for the best?'

4. Use humour and fun. This is a most delightful *kingdom reversal*: instead of anxiety being reduced by extensive self and group analysis and intensive heart-searching, anxiety is lifted by fun and laughter. In anxious situations laughter is, to use Peter Berger's expression, a 'rumour of angels'. Unfortunately, when people are caught up in the bad habits of herding and distancing the last thing on the agenda is play and laughter. The wise leader recognizes that the rhythm of a healthy community has to involve time for play and laughter, even if they do not consider themselves to be good at contributing humour and playfulness[7].

As well as specific practices and habits that can be adopted to help prevent the stoking up of anxiety, it is important to develop the capacity to be a 'non-anxious presence'. This skill is essential to the leader of worship, the convenors of public meetings as well as the community chaplain. This ability is hugely important and straightforward to achieve – with a modicum of practice. First it involves logging our own anxiety. Only when we can sense and track our own anxiety do we have any chance of reducing it. Then it is possible to 'park' that anxiety – consciously putting it out of the way. Somewhere in our brains there is a space that can hold anxiety in a way that limits its interference. There is a Buddhist practice that can help us locate that anxiety 'parking space'. It involves *softening* our eyes. When we are anxious our eyes become hard and they also look hard, hence the expressions 'Stop eyeballing me' or 'Get out of my face'.

We can tell the level of our anxiety by checking our eyes. You can't do fury with soft eyes. Kids know the extent to which they can push you by the softness – or hardness – of your eyes. When we soften our eyes we immediately increase the likelihood of responding calmly rather than reacting with our cold-blooded, reptile brain. Buddhists recommend that softening the eyes becomes part of the discipline of prayer-fulness. It is part of the quietening that helps us to be more open to God – and to each other. For those who are bemused by the bidding to soften our eyes there is one final clue to the process. If it is difficult to find that mental and muscular process that enables us to soften our eyes then look upon a new-born baby. Our eyes soften and our hearts moisten. This would seem to be yet another gracious gift that has come from our Heavenly Father who knows all too well what desperately anxious creatures we are.

Community chaplain – the skills

The community chaplain has to know about anxiety, and how to handle anxious people and anxious situations. However, there are other skills that the community chaplain needs. The community chaplain always remains a visitor to the groups using the church community centre. This means that he or she has to respect the autonomy of the groups and the groups' leaders. This calls for the skill that Adam Smith articulated as far back as 1759, it involves 'endeavour[ing] to put himself [sic] in the situation of the other, and to bring home to himself every little circumstance of distress which can possibly occur to [the other person] ... in its minutest incidents'[8]. Sympathy requires the capacity to perceive and feel those 'minutest incidents', but the challenge to the community minister goes beyond empathy and sympathy. The challenge is to balance sympathy that might be felt for the person with the autonomy of the person. The community chaplain must not 'reduce' that person to a recipient of their concern. Before the community chaplain can offer anything (other than personal and private prayer) trust has to have been established.

The community chaplain has to be skilled at respecting boundaries and, in some instances, maintaining boundaries. The challenge at the heart of the role is to create and maintain a porous and delicate membrane that prevents caring and being alongside drifting into controlling and shaping. This is why it is important to distinguish the idea of chaplain from that of minister. The community chaplain has to let go of any desire to shape or control how people think, both about their neighbours and God. To breach or destroy this membrane would be to cut across the hospitality which the church centre represents. The foundational domain is about helping people to sense the possibility of God. It is also about rehabilitating the Church in people's minds. Hospitality and generosity in response to people's expressed needs are important elements in this process of rehabilitation.

However, there remains the potentially vexed issue of how and when we do try to introduce people to the unique and saving grace of God through Jesus? Here the maturity and integrity of the community chaplain is essential. The membrane between care and control is porous, allowing the chaplain to speak from her or his own experience. This may be labelled by some as witnessing. However, the effectiveness of 'witnessing' is closely related to the ability of the speaker to speak not from a position of strength but from a position of vulnerability. It is the sharing of occasions where we have feared being overwhelmed that creates the bond of trust, and only when this bond has been created can the message of salvation be heard and understood.

There are opportunities to invite and even expect people to pray. For example, the invitation to pray for the very ill, young daughter of the woman who runs the keep fit would likely gain a very positive response. The community chaplain might even draft a short prayer to be handed to people if they find it difficult to pray using their own words. The aim is to legitimize prayer as a normal response to distress, and to talk about prayer openly and as a matter of fact, just as one might talk of a night out. Praying causes people to move from a God who exists 'out there' to God who is alongside. Prayer is our way of embracing the intimacy of God. By encouraging and enabling people to pray an important bridge is provided between the foundational and explicit domains.

The list of skills and aptitudes needed for a community chaplain may appear quite daunting, especially as the role is voluntary. However, the skills are about being a decent human being who has taken up God's offer of intimacy and who retains an open and convivial perspective alongside this realistic faith. So the person specification might read:

♦ Able to create an 'upbeat' atmosphere
♦ Able to create warm and trusting relations with a wide range of people
♦ Able to speak from a questing yet tested faith
♦ Able to speak from a position of vulnerability
♦ Able to hold confidences
♦ Able to organize events/social activity encouraging the involvement of others
♦ Able to host opportunities for reflection on current/local issues from a faith perspective
♦ Able to maintain a realistic and considered boundary especially in relation to pastoral issues
♦ Able to give three hours a week, either daytime, evenings or over the weekend

Ideally a church might have two or three community chaplains so that they can work to each other's strengths, and cover for each other's weaknesses, just like any team might.

It is essential that supervision and support are provided regularly for the community chaplains. The supervision provided for community chaplains would need to be attentive to the boundary issues that the role needs to maintain, for example in relation to confidentiality; pastoral issues that have been identified and recognizing the different responses that may be possible; talking through contacts and relationships that feel dodgy or provoke concern; identifying the scope for apt liturgy and other specific events and identifying occasions for greater integration between church and community. Supervision will also be an occasion for praying for the issues that the community chaplain has raised and for praying for the community chaplain directly.

Church community centres = A church with many congregations

It is stating the obvious to say that the community chaplain role helps bridge the gap between church and community. However, this begs the question what is the difference between the congregation and, say, the lunch club for old people or the whist drive? Could it be that the difference is more in our minds than it is in reality? Could the boundary between the two categories be more pervious than we realize?

Take for example an Oasis Group. This is an approach recommended by Rhena Taylor in relation to work with older people. The Oasis Group is for those who have moved from their third age to their fourth age, the stage of relinquishing. The Oasis is a 'holiday at home' for those who no longer feel able to go away for a week's holiday. It might involve one of the rooms in the church centre being adapted for a week to look as much as possible like a palm court or hotel lounge. People are collected by car and brought to the mock hotel lounge for morning coffee followed by a short trip, a tea dance or a musical performance. Lunch is served and so too is afternoon tea. After this the person is taken home by car. On the Sunday an invitation is issued to join in worship followed by lunch.

When harvest supper comes round members of the Oasis Group receive a special invitation with transport provided and likewise at Christmas there is a reunion lunch for everyone. The model provided 'episodes' of support and activity.

This episodic approach has much to commend it. It is easier to get a group of volunteers together to organize a special event than it is for something that takes place each week or fortnight. It also creates a sense of anticipation, and having something to look forward to is a powerful antidote to melancholy. Furthermore, episodic approaches to social action do not carry the same risk of drifting into 'needs meeting'. It remains something special rather than routine, and retains an essential 'I – Thou' relationship more effectively than regular provision, where over time the 'I – It' relationship that talks of clients and users is hard to resist.

The role of the community chaplain in relation to an Oasis Group might be:

♦ Identifying, approaching and supporting the coordinators and providers of the 'Oasis' and praying with and for them.
♦ Based on previous networking, overseeing liaison with providers of support for elderly people in the locality to identify those who might be pleased to receive an invitation to the 'holiday at home'.
♦ Popping into the events hosted during the week and chatting with people. Possibly asking if they have any prayer requests that the church can support. The direct question 'What sort of things are you praying for?' may not go amiss – probably 70 per cent of those in their fourth age pray regularly. It is not the end of the world if the response is 'No thank you. I don't go in for that sort of thing'. Furthermore, the skill at saying 'no' is well honed by the time a person has reached their fourth age.
♦ Inviting the organizers of the Oasis week to meet to evaluate how things had worked out and to consider what next.
♦ Plugging gaps in the arrangements – acting as first backstop.
♦ Being alert to funding opportunities for Oasis 'holiday at home' and alerting the coordinator to these.

This list of possibilities highlights how the role of community chaplain enables a group to develop a spiritual dimension and to enable members of the group to sense that they are part of a church network. The episodic nature of the activities prevents people feeling overwhelmed, or in an 'all or nothing' relationship with the church. The community chaplain's role enables attention to detail which helps people to feel they are significant. This is so important for people who are easily dismissed or disparaged. Part of the art of the chaplain's role is to generate an atmosphere that takes praying and doing business with God as a normal, routine activity, thus enabling people to come out of the closet as regards their spirituality and sense of the presence of God. Before long it becomes possible to invite members of the group to a parish weekend, to an Alpha course or even to confirmation classes. On a very basic level one speculates that a collection box labelled 'For the ministry of the church in this place' will receive donations and these donations will be shown in the church's annual accounts as 'giving from the Oasis Group'.

So does the Oasis Group and other groups using the church centre count as a congregation? Certainly the group provides a hugely effective foundation for the explicit domain. But more than this, those associated with the group are likely to feel that they come away from the 'oasis' having received more than they had expected. Coming away with more than one anticipated is as close a definition of receiving a blessing as one can get. Receiving blessings, receiving and giving support to others and having one's eyes lifted above the horizon of the routine is not a bad list of criteria for a congregation. The distinction between groups using the church centre and the Sunday congregation may not be as great as we imagine. In fact the biggest gap between the two may be a product of our own failure of imagination and failure to 'think outside the box'.

Notes

1 Community centres run by local authorities are often 'stop – go' depending on the amount of spare cash that the local authority has in its coffers. It is a rare local authority which consistently allocates high priority to the funding of a community centre when cuts are being taken by social services or schools. Often tenants' or community associations resort to running a bar in their community centres in order to ensure sufficient income. Unfortunately the community centre can easily degenerate into a drinking club, and this works against the centre being welcoming to all sections of the community.

2 For example racist groups are likely to have their request to hire facilities declined.

3 'Impression management' and 'unmeant gestures' are terms used by Irvine Goffman in his classic book on symbol interactionism, *The Presentation of Self in Everyday Life* (London: The Penguin Press, 1969).

4 This is a term used by Jonathan Draper, Canon Theologian at York Minster in *Cross Currents*, 'Religion and Intellectual Life', Winter 1990–1, pp. 541–7, quotation on p. 547.

5 In a legalistic culture it would be wise to make reference to the role of the community chaplain in the hiring agreement or its attachments. For example: community chaplains are local people who have received training and are supervised in relation to their role and have been vetted for the protection of children and vulnerable adults. Reference also needs to be made to how the hirer of the facilities can raise any concerns or complaints they might have in relation to the community chaplain.

6 Training might include: the principles and practice of community development; networking; apt liturgy; government policies in relation to social inclusion; social capital; models of mission; faith development.

7 When personal anxiety levels are reduced our inclination

to play and aptitude to generate fun and laughter all increase, not least because our ability to laugh at ourselves increases, and laughing at ourselves is probably the safest route with which the novice can begin to generate laughter!

8 Adam Smith, *The Theory of Moral Sentiments* (Indianapolis: Liberty Fund Press, 1982), p. 21.

10

The Vocational Domain

As a kid I was encouraged to think that it wasn't just Jesus who walked on water, Bill Shankley could as well. Red was my colour and Liverpool my team. Having been nurtured on football I cannot escape seeing the model of holistic mission that I espouse as being that of centre forward, supported by right and left wingers. The centre forward (Michael Owen is his name) relies on getting good service from the wingers. Without this his capacity for scoring is hugely weakened. This is also how it is in relation to a strategy for holistic mission. In a post-Christendom context the explicit domain is greatly weakened unless it is served by the foundational and vocational wings.

To stay with the football analogy (don't worry not for very long!), the Church pays big money for the centre forwards who operate in the explicit domain (that is clergy, ministers and the administrative structures that shore up our way of being church). The foundational wing is beginning to make a few helpful passes, but the same is yet to be said for the vocational wing. The absence of specialist work in relation to the vocational domain is a major weakness in the development of holistic mission. It is the work we do on the vocational wing that has the greatest potential for transformation not just of the Church but also of our communities and the habits of people.

The vocational domain is about encouraging people to discover and embrace their vocation – their distinctive call from God. Vocation is for people outside the Church as much as those within, and for non-Christians as much as for Christians. This is a radical departure from how the idea of vocation is used within our churches. Vocation has become restricted to the elite of our churches: people test their vocation to the priesthood or, less commonly, to a religious order, or they go to Methodist Conference to have their call to ministry considered. Given this narrowing of the idea of vocation it is tempting to abandon the terminology because of the risk of it being misunderstood. However the alternative terminology – that of discipleship – is equally contaminated. Discipleship and disciples are terms which belong to the close followers of Jesus, whether in the time of Jesus himself or today. Discipleship is the serious business that is a measure of one's commitment as a Christian. Rather than these elite understandings of vocation and discipleship, holistic mission calls for vocation and discipleship to be open to all, for the response to the call from within to be more and better than we are and is a democratic, all-including, human phenomenon. By enabling people to heed and respond to this calling within them, people both work for the kingdom of God and discover God – and this is the very thing that holistic mission seeks to achieve.

The justification of this big claim requires a distinction between 'doing jobs in church' and discipleship. Karl Rahner's recoding of the term discipleship as venturesome love enables a clearer assessment of what is and what is not discipleship. Discipleship as an expression of venturesome love implies that an element of risk-taking is involved in relation to concern for the other person. Unfortunately, most church life revolves around running the church, to the extent that the normative model of how one expresses deeper commitment to God is by ever greater involvement in running the church. This uncritical focus on the internal life of the church is usually at the expense of risk-taking on behalf of the well-being of the other. The cost of this is the loss of the essential dynamic which unites the growth of faith and the struggle for the Kingdom of God.

Moral-selving

Underpinning the notion of risk-taking for the sake of others is the business of morality. Morality is a straightforward concept. It means actions by human agents and how those actions impinge on others and on the world. Just as power is always present in a situation or encounter so too is morality. In a post-modern world the continuities of life and ability to understand the rules of the game evaporate. However, the idea that in a post-modern context there is a moral vacuum is misleading. Rather we have a situation of moral autonomy and the consequences of this are huge. The loneliness and uncertainty that surround the choices that one makes can be debilitating, for it is no easy matter to respond to a situation in a way that measures up to one's self-image in a context that lauds freedom of choice and the right of everyone to walk away from moral commitment. With no agreed foundation for values and ethics each of us is confronted with the reality of our own moral autonomy and our 'own non-get-riddable, inalienable moral responsibility'.[1] This is an uncomfortable and uneasy situation in which to be, to the extent that Bauman describes it as 'moral agony'.[2] The Church has yet to take seriously the demands that people face in trying to find and express a moral commitment (not to be confused with moral opinions) in this context of permissive fragmentation and discontinuity. This is an urgent pastoral challenge to the Church as much as it is a challenge to holistic mission.

The task of helping people to develop a moral self today is profoundly different from the task with which the Church is familiar. Church practice has historically concentrated on urging people to act within the explicit rules of moral behaviour. The Church was guided in this historic task by the moral philosophy expressed by Thomas Hobbes: if people are to be moral they have to be forced to be so, and this calls for both a constraining and a punitive force. The Church's efforts at constraining people's behaviour today get deservedly mocked. A new approach to 'moral-selving' is required. This new approach has to enable people to discover for themselves a moral or value base that they can embrace and it involves providing structures by which people can act on this morality.

In the past one could express one's values or morals through one's occupation, especially by employment in the public or health services. Bauman suggests this option is no longer available. He comments, 'If anything, they make the life of the stubbornly moral person tough and unrewarding.'[3] Defensive bureaucracy increasingly frustrates the expression of public service, and the preoccupation with short-term performance measures likewise inhibits the scope for expressing one's moral self.

The formation and expression of a distinctive moral identity is an important aspect of the journey towards individuation, but such a journey embarked upon without support carries a health warning. The sheer heroism involved in separating ourselves from the crowd and living a life which has both integrity and courage, Becker, along with other depth psychologists, suggests constitutes so demanding a task that it will likely drive the individual mad. But despite the impossibility of achieving this separation from the shaping and constraining forces of one's environment, the call towards heroism from deep within persists. Becker warns that this calling towards being something more, to the extent of being heroic, can tempt the person to respond with ever more introspection. But this is the route to madness; according to Becker it is a mistake to try to surmount the confusion, doubt and hesitation associated with the outset of the process towards individuation by philosophizing and thinking. Rather it is by acting and engaging that resolution can come. A task for the vocational domain is to provide some structure to facilitate the engagement that is essential to the development of a coherent and authentic moral self which is so important to the journey of individuation.

The term 'moral-selving' is used by Rebecca Anne Allahyari in her study of volunteers working with the Catholic Worker Movement and the Salvation Army in the USA. Her research provides insights about how to help people to 'craft' or foster within themselves a more virtuous and, often, more spiritual self.[4] The moral preferences, decisions and actions that we opt for are the product of the environments in which we find ourselves. In other words, constructing or crafting our moral selves involves *collecting* moral ideas, from individual encounters. The implication of our moral self being malleable or changeable is that there is scope for all of us to craft a more virtuous self. However, this in turn raises a further issue, especially when the prevailing opinion is that we are becoming less and less concerned with behaving in a moral way. Just how robust is the motivation to craft a moral self? Could we have lost the motivation to behave in moral ways?

In chapter 8 the idea of *adaequatio* was referred to (when discussing the capacity for sensing the reality of God). *Adaequatio* refers to the instruments of recognition that enable us to 'receive' or perceive the outside world. In relation to moral-selving the question becomes *have we got it in us* to make a commitment to being moral? The answer comes from the most acclaimed post-modern ethicist, Emmanuel Lévinas. He suggests, in fact insists, that all of us possess the fundamental capacity as human beings for *encounter with the face of the other*.[5] It is this virtually biological capacity, which exists prior to any teaching or social conventions, that is the foundation of moral behaviour. It is the face of the other which provokes the sentiment which prefigures moral behaviour.

This deep capacity for seeing the face of the other does not present a road map that can guide our actions, but it does offer something quite profound. In a post-modern context where the rules of the games have evaporated, the encounter with the face of the other enriches both parties, because in acting without the guidance of convention or command we encounter each other with faces free of any masks, and through this we also meet or discover our own bare or naked face. The relationship or encounter is profoundly personal, and in responding we see ourselves in a way which discloses our identity to both ourselves and others.

In a post-modern world the prompt to moral-selving is an encounter with the face of the other[6] and our post-modern world supplies a further motivation to craft a more moral self. In a context where moral rules and social norms have eroded or become fragmented, we enter a state where our proficiencies and potencies evaporate. Confronted by an inability to know what to do for the best, other than to organize life around selfishness, 'We shiver in the nakedness of nihilism in which near-omnipotence is paired with near-emptiness, greatest capacity [is paired] with knowing least what for.'[7] It may provide sufficient motivation to embrace the task of moral-selving just to avoid this desperate state. It is of course possible to protect ourselves from such nakedness by embracing all kinds of trivial or Philistine behaviour such as Kierkegaard warns against. Likewise, religious believers who embrace their faith with an unwarranted certainty adopt a similarly protective technique. The holding on to right answers is a very effective method of protecting one's self from the moral agony to which Bauman refers. The problem with this protective technique is that it inhibits fraternal relations with those who maintain a different and, possibly, opposing set of right answers. In the global village that the world has become, to maintain a protective strategy which leads to an inability to be open-handed in relation to different views and ideology is itself less than moral. It is also at odds with the urgings and example that Jesus provides.

Truth is relational

The insight that Jesus offers us is that truth and moral commitment are essential to each other, to the extent that they cannot and should not be separated. This is what Jesus both preached and practised. Our Christian faith is rooted in a person who said 'I am ... the truth'. Jesus did not say 'I will speak true words to you' or 'I will tell you about the truth'. Instead, the claim Jesus makes is that He embodies truth in His person. Palmer, reflecting on Jesus' claim, comments that 'Those who sought truth were invited into relationship with him and through him with the whole community of the human and non-human world.'[8] This view of truth rejects the idea that truth is an objective 'out there', but rather understands truth as something that comes to be known through encounter and relationship. This linking of encounter and truth is a fundamental insight that Jesus urges us to test and embrace. It is also a remarkably apposite perspective for our post-modern context, for it is the very perspective that Lévinas posits.

The challenge we face is not about being hospitable to other ideas, other beliefs or claims of moral truth. The challenge is to be open or hospitable to other relationships or encounters, for relationships, not facts and reason, are key to unfurling truth. This leads Palmer to conclude that 'If what we *know* is an abstract, impersonal, apart from us, it cannot be truth, for truth involves a vulnerable, faithful, and risk filled interpenetration of the knower and the known.'[9] Thus the task of moral-selving, which calls us to be open and responsive to others, is a task which supports journeying towards Godly truth.

Work in the vocational domain involves providing structures which enable people to embark on relationships as a way of knowing enduring truth. This is a startlingly different approach to mission from that which is usually adopted. However it is consistent with the new understanding of moral reality that Lévinas expounds – as well as being consistent with what Jesus both proclaimed and incarnated. Thus the quality of our relationships and encounters are not just about ethics and morality, they also provide us with an epistemology, i.e. a way of knowing profound and transforming truth. A danger with this approach to seeking after truth is that it disintegrates into an expression of our private perceptions and inclinations. This kind of subjectivism is disappointing as well as a cul-de-sac. If our private perceptions become the measure of truth, and if my truth cannot be contested or enlarged by another, I have merely found one more way to objectify and keep at arm's length the challenge of new ways of seeing.

Palmer writes, 'Truth is between us, in relationship, to be found in dialogue of knowers and knowns who are understood as independent but accountable selves.'[10] The accountability that Palmer refers to means listening without power, for accountability means ceding power to the 'other' and resisting the inclination to diminish or limit 'the other' to self-serving images.[11] It means experiencing 'the other' without imposing our prejudgements and suppositions. Truth that has its roots in relationship does not lead to individualism and subjectivism but seeks encounter with those who are different from us and who see things differently from us. Truth, therefore, is neither 'out there' nor 'in here', but rather it is both these things. Dialogue means being open to the possibility of being changed by what the other discloses.

Work in the vocational domain aims to enable people to embark on relationships as a way of knowing enduring truth. To do this requires that we take seriously the breadth of fraternal relations that unfurl before us as a result of sharing the same Heavenly Father. James Alison explores this idea of our limitless, fraternal relations and from this a radical reading of the Gospels unfolds. He suggests that the essence of Jesus' teaching is that in accepting the graceful offer of God as our Father we also embrace fraternal relations beyond our family. Furthermore we are urged by Jesus to stretch out to those who have no belonging and shun earthbound understandings of fraternal relations because an earthbound view of fraternity limits our relationship to those most like ourselves. Alison doesn't mince his words, he calls this craving for the like-minded as *idolatrous belonging*.[12] This injunction against idolatry is one that we need to revisit because of its relevance to our post-modern world. To treat the familiar and the local as if they were absolute, as if they are the be-alls and end-alls of value is the sin of idolatry. Idolatry, like sloth, is a capital or deadly sin that spawns pathological religion, pathological politics and pathological communities.

Community ministry and the vocational domain

For the sake of the health of communities, faiths, civil society and the Creation, the Church has three very urgent tasks:

♦ to provide encouragement and opportunity for people to develop or 'craft' a more moral self;
♦ to provide encouragement and opportunity for people to express fraternal relations beyond the limits of family, household or the like-minded;
♦ to provide opportunities for people to encounter the face of 'the other' and the face of Jesus that enables a journey towards Godly truth.

These are the objectives of the vocational domain. The method or means of meeting these objectives is not arduous, in fact it is both near to hand and, as is so often the case with God's gracious economy, the means of achieving these objectives may also trigger many other virtuous outcomes. The means of delivering on these objectives is by providing structures (i.e. supported opportunities) that enable people *to encounter the face of the other* in a profound and potentially transforming way.

Those who participate in community ministry do so with little power. As volunteers they possess neither the status nor capacity to shape outcomes or the behaviour of others. All the volunteer can do is to draw alongside and listen – without power. The absence of power can bring grace, the grace that enables an 'I - Thou' relationship to grow in contrast to the objectifying and diminishing relationship of 'I - It'.[13] Being without power when alongside those who know deeply about struggle can be distressing and even harrowing. It involves the risk of being overwhelmed and the possibility of losing control. For there are no limits to what to the distress and suffering one might discover.

Even without such an emotionally challenging encounter, involvement in community ministry confronts the participant with the unfamiliar, and this interrupts our sense of being in control. In allowing ourselves to be without power in a challenging situation or encounter we open ourselves to a *thin place*, where something new and something with a moral imperative can intrude. In looking into the face of the old woman with dementia we see our own potential self. Listening without power to the man struggling with schizophrenia as he expresses his confidence in God's protection provokes an internal conversation within the listener to which he or she will likely return on many occasions. Inviting the suburban husband and wife to journey to Manila provokes within each of them an internal conversation which forces them to confront their inclination to be timid – or courageous. Seeing the face of the asylum seeker who is alone in a strange land evokes within us a recognition of our own vulnerability and our shared need for human companionship. In contrast to these insights, those who possess the power in a relationship are prone to be locked into their own assumptions and see only their own version of truth. The imperialism that so often besets the powerful means that an encounter with 'the other' rarely carries this epistemological potential.

At a minimum, involvement in community ministry and the encounters that result provoke an internal or interior conversation within the participant. Such internal pondering is an important feature of the vocational domain. The internal conversation might be generated around questions such as 'What should I do for the best?', 'Could I?', 'Should I?' These are questions that go right to the heart of vocational and moral behaviour. Such heartfelt pondering should not be underestimated, because it prefigures humility within the questioner. Humility 'is an attitude toward facts and messages outside oneself; an openness to experience as well as to criticism; and a sensitivity and responsiveness to the needs and concerns of others'.[14] Humility involves a profoundly sceptical attitude to one's own ability in relation to the demands one faces. Humility is critical to the vocational domain for it makes us ready for inner reassessment and inner rearrangement associated with encountering new learning and information.

A cascade of grace

Willingness to be alongside those who know deeply about struggle, are without power and are aware of the possibility of being overwhelmed is what venturesome love is all about. Community ministry involves the provision of structures that enable people to express venturesome love, and with this comes a number of other positive outcomes, some of which are particularly relevant to contemporary pressures and anxieties. For example:

- the scope to 'practise' or rehearse the possibility of being overwhelmed provides an important therapeutic contribution that enables a more open recognition of personal vulnerability in an intensely narcissistic culture;
- the opening of people's minds to the possibility of insights from the most unlikely sources, bringing greater inclination for dialogue and willingness to be changed by what one hears;
- the commitment to engage in struggle on behalf of those outside one's own household or interest group is vitally important at a time when social capital, especially bridging social capital, is in such short supply;
- the invitation to the secure and comfortable to embrace a struggle and to step outside the metaphorical play-pen of the suburban household or yuppie pleasure dome is nothing less than class treason;
- the expression of commitment to those who are in need fulfils the criterion of 'authenticity' that is so important as a basis for judgement in a post-modern context.

With these kinds of positive associations it is remarkable that churches have invested so few of their core resources in developing and promoting the structures of participation associated with community ministry. This may be because of the negative overlay that social action often carries. The accusation of do-gooding still echoes, and the idea of being Lady Bountiful can still haunt. These twentieth-century epithets still have power and continue to work against active discipleship. It may be, of course, that the Church dismisses social action because it is fearful of its transformational potential.

Vocation not do-gooding

All the talk of an open-handed and transformational encounter with those who know personally the reality of struggle risks naivety. This reliance on relational encounters underestimates how charity itself can wound. People who have had a comfortable and secure life, despite their best intentions, can violate those who have been battered and bruised by hardship. Richard Sennett comments that 'Pity can beget contempt; compassion can be intimately linked with inequality. ... Crossing the boundary of inequality might require *reserve* on the part of the stronger person making the passage.'[15] Sennett suggests that reserve is a sign of respect of the more lowly in the relationship because it is an acknowledgement of the difficulty they will have in making sense of the motivation of the powerful to enter into such a relationship. The reserve allows for the lowly to reflect on 'Why are you interested in me?'; 'Why are you so keen on commitment and wanting to help me?' For those coming from a position of relative power there is a real tension between expressing commitment and the fear of giving offence. How do we cross the boundary of inequality and achieve mutual respect? There is a challenge here that cannot and should not be ducked.

The powerful have to grant autonomy to the less powerful in the relationship. This involves accepting what one does not understand. The acceptance that one cannot understand things about another gives both standing and equality in the relationship. Allowing the weaker in the encounter to retain autonomy permits both connection and strangeness, closeness and freedom.[16] The unwillingness to grant autonomy can characterize much of the professional practice of welfare agencies. Failure to allow autonomy into the relationship rapidly permeates our orientation and our language, and just like Lady Bountiful and the do-gooder, we begin to treat the poor like faulty goods or seconds. Allowing autonomy is an essential characteristic of hospitality and it is why hospitality is a radical rather than puny or condescending act.

There is another difficulty about crossing the boundary of inequality. Intuitively, both parties in the encounter will sense that a characteristic of the powerful is that in contrast to the powerless, they have faith in their own future. It is for this reason that being confronted by the possibility of being overwhelmed that can beset the powerful when encountering those who know deeply about struggle is so important. It invites the powerful to let go of the well-practised habit of presenting themselves in public as 'sorted' and omnicompetent rather than vulnerable and fearful of being overwhelmed. When the powerful can achieve this stripping of pretence there is openness to a graceful moment when we discover that by loving the vulnerable we have learned to love ourselves, and may be even to love God.

And another difficulty: the anthropologist, Mary Douglas, observes that charity can wound because a freely-given gift can impose a heavy burden of gratitude on the recipient whose only way of response might be that of submission. Douglas argues that mutual respect requires some kind of reciprocity.[17] Largesse, which ignores reciprocity, has the capacity to manipulate and corrupt. Furthermore, and more offensively, compassion and charity can become a substitute for justice. There is a danger that by idealizing encounter and empathetic compassion we avoid the possibility that something more radical is required. However, an encounter, even between those unequal in power and resources, can prompt solidarity and indignation. These are expressions of mutuality, and they can embolden *both* parties in the encounter, and these sentiments make the call for justice more likely as well as more robust.

There is an even more damning critique of reliance on the *face of the other* to enable one to craft one's moral self. This critique is expressed most fully by Hannah Arendt. She suggests that coopting the other on behalf on one's own personal development is to treat others as 'mere occasions'. Arendt suggests the key question to be posed of the powerful in the relationship or encounter is 'Why are you helping me?' Arendt suspected that the powerful would be unable to answer this question without exposing their self-preoccupation and self-interest.[18] This potential, or indeed actual, instrumentality that underpins moral-selving would seem to betray an 'I - It' relationship that lurks within an apparently 'I - Thou' encounter. Such duplicity is not unusual in human relations. Ultimately, we have to choose for ourselves the extent to which we go with Arendt's negative view of humanity. If it is the case that our efforts at compassion risk injuring because of impure motives the question becomes what is the alternative? To *resist* a response of sympathy and commitment because of the fear of having mixed motives? Furthermore, what does 'help' look like without the potential of an *encounter* with the other, and does care which denies the possibility of encounter have anything to commend it?

The democratic fact of life: All have sinned

This inherent inequality in the encounter between the poor and struggling with the *apparently* secure and confident cannot and should not be brushed aside. Therefore, in equipping people to cross the boundary of inequality that is such an essential aspect of the vocational domain the Church must encourage people to willingly embrace humility and honest scrutiny. The most effective way of achieving this is by ensuring there are opportunities for people to reflect on their experiences and their encounters associated with their involvement in social action. Through this reflection comes an increased awareness of our sinfulness. The growth in awareness of our sinfulness is vitally important to the challenge of crossing the boundary of inequality.

The basis of solidarity between those who are unequal in terms of power is in relation to our spiritual status: for *all* have sinned and fallen short. The great democratic fact of our very existence is that of our sinfulness. Helping people to recognize sin is not such an impossible task, for one of the unexpected outcomes of community ministry is the increased capacity for theological insight.

> I suspect I started to volunteer to serve breakfast to the homeless as a way of being a more faithful disciple. I did not volunteer to have my heart broken. However, at the basement door I have come not to a greater confidence in my own good works, but to a deeper awareness of my personal sins and my complicity in sinful systems, as well as to a greater dependence on the grace of Jesus Christ.
>
> In many ways the basement door is a joyful place – a place of handshakes and conversation and fellowship. However, the door also brings with it times of conflict and, almost always, a sense of failure and a glimpse of the cross. The person working the door is the one who has to say 'No, you can't come in yet ... there's no room at the tables' ... 'No, you're too late, we're not serving breakfast any more'.
>
> What a revelation this has been! I had always assumed that discipleship followed the confession of sin and the acceptance of forgiveness. The faltering hospitality offered via the basement door has taught me that the process is actually reversed: we do not fully know the depth of our sin and the reality of God's grace until we follow the way of Jesus.[19]

This reflection is provided by Saunders and Campbell, both of whom are professors of theology who chose to spend a sabbatical working as volunteers in shelters for the homeless. They articulate the significance of the vocational domain: it is a route to recognizing our need for a saviour. This is the second reason why helping people to recognize sin and think, and even speak, in terms of sin is an important task for the vocational domain. It is because it prepares the ground for the message of forgiveness that is so essential to the explicit domain where the message of salvation is unambiguously proclaimed.

How realistic is all this?

The vocational domain is about encouraging and enabling people to express discipleship, regardless of whether they are Christian. The significance of the vocational domain in relation to the Church's missionary task is that it overthrows the usual 'belonging, believing, behaving' formula and presumes that the expression of venturesome love can be a route to faith and not just an expression of faith. Furthermore, this distinctive journey to faith generates attributes that are vitally important in a world were hardwired beliefs are a liability. In a diverse world, faith as opposed to belief is called for as a basis for healthy religion. Faith that has been nourished by humility and an epistemology that expects difference to be a source of insight rather than threat is to be preferred over a process that leaves people bound by belief. If the prize that awaits as a result of investing in the vocational domain is a tolerant but tested commitment to Jesus as saviour and teacher, then the only justification for failing to make such an investment is that the approach proves unviable because of people's lack of interest. However, the evidence suggests that this is far from likely to be the case.

In Chapter 5 (p. 106) the development of a market for 'experiences' propounded by Pine and Gilmore was explored. As we reach satiation in relation to 'stuff' (commodities and products) our interest shifts towards experiences and, in particular, transformational experiences. Pine and Gilmore write, 'Transformations are a distinctive economic offering, they form the final, i.e. the highest aspect of progression of economic value. A transformation is what the out-of-shape person, the emotionally troubled person, the young managers, the hospital patient and the struggling company all really desire.'[20] It is transformational experiences that people really aspire to and Pine and Gilmore recommend that forward-looking businesses need to organize themselves to take advantage of this shift in market trends. In support of this analysis Virginia Postrel comments 'We are in fact living more and more in an intangible economy, in which the greatest sources of wealth are not physical. We aren't yet used to an economy in which beauty, amusement, attention, learning, pleasure, even spiritual fulfilment are as real and as economically valuable as steel or semiconductors.'[21] This analysis emphasizes the viability and significance of the Church increasing its commitment to work in the vocational domain and to compete in the emerging market. After all, the Church is the original purveyor of transformational experiences.

It is oddly reassuring that the world is catching up with the processes that the Church has nurtured and honed for centuries. It is also encouraging to see how the process of fostering transformation is depicted by those who are marketing wizards. For example, those who seek to purchase experiences are referred to as 'aspirants' because they *aspire* to be someone different from how they perceive themselves. Those who buy experiences are explicitly seeking an opportunity to express and practise a change in attitude, performance, personal characteristics or other fundamental dimensions of their lives. The word 'aspirant' is traditionally used by those who are in the first stage of testing their vocation to a religious order. Not for the first time the secular world has adopted a religious concept in order to express the profoundness of what is being marketed within the experience economy.

There is further encouragement for the Church as Pine and Gilmore identify the characteristics of the much sought after 'sweet spot' where a number of factors come together and increase the likelihood of transformation. The four realms of experience that constitute a sweet spot for transformation are:

♦ experiences that alter our view of the world;
♦ experiences that help us rethink how we fit into that world;
♦ experiences that boost our personal capabilities and characteristics to new levels;
♦ experiences that imbue a sense of wonder, beauty and appreciation.[22]

There could scarcely be a better description of what the vocational domain offers to people in their drive to craft a moral self.

Not copying – contesting!

The purpose of learning from those who wish to push the market system to its zenith is not to urge the Church into accepting such predatory and personalized practices. Rather, the increased assurance that the Church can derive from this emerging experience economy must enable the Church to contest more effectively this highly significant arena. Just as there is cheap grace so too there is cheap transformation. Cheap transformation comes in the shape of the latest vodka mix or an ecstasy tablet. There is a generation that is so hooked on the chemical route to transformation that the possibility of a journey to moral-selving and moral responsibility is undermined. The urge for a story-rich life can be achieved as much through Ibiza nights as it can through digging wells with Africans. The structures that give access to the story-riches of the Costa del Sol or Aya Napa are alive and well. The adverts in the window of the high street travel agency couldn't make it easier. In contrast, the person with an inclination towards the challenge of moral-selving requires utter determination and thorough research to locate the structures that might enable them to achieve the transformation they seek.

Given that the Church and associated agencies are the original dealers in transformations it would be irresponsible to ignore a market that is rampantly seeking transformational experience. Following the lead of the business world the Church has to become proactive in its dealings with people, unafraid of the fact that people don't know clearly what it is they wish to achieve through transformation. The business world knows and understands that their customers often do not know or cannot articulate what they want. So too with aspirants, they often cannot articulate their hopes and dreams.[23] This vagueness in relation to the urge towards transformation provides the platform for the contest between kingdom-directed transformation and cheap transformation.

The paucity of models other than those that promote cheap transformations is a gap that the Church has a responsibility to address. To do this requires the provision of 'pre-formation activities' to 'first fortify the aspirant in those areas in which he is too weak to proceed'[24]. This could be a description of what is often referred to as pre-evangelism. However, in the vocational domain the task is to fortify the inclination towards moral-selving and this needs to take a different shape. A good example of this is the annual pilgrimage between London and Canterbury organized by St Martin's-in-the-Fields for both homeless and housed. The boast on the flier reads 'Once you've done it, you just have to come back next year ... and the next ... and the next'. The pilgrimage offers that 'sweet spot' that Pine and Gilmore highlight. It also provides that combination of convivial partnership, and easy-going spirituality and carries story-rich potential. The offer of partaking in a 'bank holiday weekend of a lifetime' is precisely the kind of preformative experience that 'fortifies' the aspirant to continue to clarify the nature of the transformation that he or she seeks.

There are other examples of pre-formative experiences that churches and church-related agencies are starting to develop. Camden in North London is perhaps the most expressively post-modern location in Britain.[25] The churches in the borough have had to adapt themselves to this market-leading community. At St Michael's, Camden Town, six years ago the congregation was down to single figures and the listed building near derelict. The building is still in need of renovation but the congregation is vibrant and Camden Town is aware that it has a church in its community that is relevant and as full of life as the community itself. The church is unafraid of doing things 'large', wanting to have an impact, whether it is by means of the jazz band that leads church processions, the mystery plays that take place in the battered gothic church or the opera singer or artist from the congregation who work with the local centre for homeless people, passing on their skills and artistry. There are events like this by the score. These are low-threshold, easy-to-access events that provide a taster of experiences that speaks of potential transformation and access to a story-rich life.

St George the Martyr in Holborn has also faced the challenge of building up its congregation and re-awakening the neighbourhood to its presence. Here the approach has been to focus energy on a single week, daring to suggest to the congregation that they should take a week off work and use their holiday to run activities and events within the parish. Old people's flats were spring cleaned, a shelter for homeless families was completely redecorated, after-school football tournaments hosted and invitations issued to hear a couple of bands at the 'The George', the new 'local'. This is part of a long-term strategy incorporating regular monthly projects, such as decorating the flat allocated to a family seeking asylum. The importance of this becoming a repeated event is endorsed by Pine and Gilmore, 'By staging a series of experiences, companies are better able to achieve a lasting effect on the buyer, than through an isolated event. It is the revisiting of a recurring theme, experienced through distinct and yet unified events that transforms.'[26] They go on to suggest that 'One-off experiences seldom yield a transformation offering, if there is no care there. Ensuring the aspirant achieves his aim, usually means providing a series of experiences, each guided by a constant set of principles. The first requirement for workers in a transformation business is that they truly care.'[27] Churches, even the most battered and bruised, retain a commitment to care, and this is a platform for engagement that we must trust rather than suspect.

The Soul Survivor movement has achieved this careful staging of experiences in order to show teenagers that embracing the Christian faith is not about rules and regulations, conformity and boredom and to take into account the primacy of authenticity to a post-modern generation. The direction of change that young people want to make in their lives is not governed by 'oughts' but by the urge for abundant life. The Christian Rock Band, Evanescence, went straight to No. 1 in the UK chart with their debut single 'Bring Me To Life'. Their lyric tapped into this urge for transformation and a story-rich life. The advent of a gap year between school and college or before starting work is part of this urge. Challenge and variety as well as care for each other, for the stranger and for those who are marginalized, all have to be present in the pre-formative experiences that are offered to potential aspirants. Soul*inthe*City, planned for London in summer 2004, will endeavour to pull all these strands together, and the task of doing so would stretch the organizational and imaginative skill of the most experienced of impresarios. Over 10,000 young people will descend on London and form teams to clear rubbish, remove graffiti, tidy gardens and party and pray in the evening. This initiative meets all the criteria of transformational experiences that Pine and Gilmore identify plus one more: Soul*inthe*City will probably create a 'line of memorability'.[28] That line of memorability will have to compete with the line of memorabililty generated by backpacking in Peru or working in a hotel in St Ives for six weeks over the summer. These will be the experiences that are recounted in the students' bar and feed into the internal conversations within people which are so important to the future choices that they will make.

It is interesting to see Holy Trinity, Brompton, one of the most innovative churches in Britain, is actively creating opportunities for its members to begin a process of moral-selving have invested in a structure to make this possible. This could be viewed as implementing the *belonging, believing* and *behaving formula*, but it is also possible to interpret this development as an intuitive response to the urge for an authentic, story-rich life which seeks out transformational experiences. Just as Holy Trinity, Brompton, was able to identify and respond to the niche called 'Alpha', it is possible that the School for Urban Mission and the Besom Project, as well as the extraordinary work with prisoners, are pathfinder initiatives that the wider church can learn from.

Returning to the vocational domain

The episodic, preformative events that I have described above take account of the vast number of competing models of life that people can choose, and they can do much to rehabilitate people's view of the Church. But they do more than this, they provide a glimpse of the benefits of moral-selving: by giving scope for wide, fraternal relations that make for a story-rich life. They also help contribute to the stock of social capital in a community, and because of the emphasis on fun, can play a part in dispelling anxiety at both personal and communal levels. These are important outcomes and deserve to take a high priority in relation to the Church's resources.

These episodic, participative events provide material that people can use to create a coherent life story. At some stage in our lives we sense the superficiality of personality and begin to recognize the value and significance of *character*. Character resides in aspiring to *maintain* an ideal, and self-respect depends on this.[29] Episodic events need to make room for more consistent expression of our moral self if we are to both develop character and sustain the transformation that is being sought. If the Church fails to provide opportunities for people to sustain their commitment to moral action then they will have little option but to shift their commitment to a voluntary organization or interest group.

There have been very successful initiatives that have given people the opportunity to sustain transformation: the Salvation Army and the Catholic Worker Movement established by Dorothy Day in the USA are perhaps the best known. Their capacity to harness the voluntary commitment of people in relation to social action is their defining characteristic. We need to revisit their approach in order to learn and develop new structures. For example, the mission societies could partner local churches to enable new structures of participation to be developed. However, transformation once it has occurred can degenerate unless it is followed through, and the skills held by the mission societies are needed if people are to integrate the story-rich, transformational experiences into their lives in the long term. This gives a completely new agenda for the home groups, cell churches and fellowship groups that are so extensive in church life, and not for the first time we can learn from Alcoholics Anonymous and other self-help groups that excel in the follow-through phase of transformation.

Powerful *and* oblique?

In the previous chapter the significance of religious experience to the foundational domain was discussed. Religious experience is also significant to the vocational domain. The prevalence and persistence of religious experience demonstrates that the *adeaquatio* or capacity for sensitivity and alertness to God remains in good shape. This capacity means that people remain open to the possibility of God's involvement in their lives. It is this persistent capacity for religious experience and the potency or effectiveness of an oblique route that makes the vocational domain so important to holistic mission, for it is at this point when work for the kingdom of God and the possibility of a personal relationship with Jesus come together. The significance of religious experience in the vocational domain is both powerful – and oblique. It is not often that the words powerful *and* oblique are linked.

Oblique usually implies indirect and therefore any impact is weakened. This powerfully oblique route associated with the vocational domain goes like this:

- Religious experience opens people to a transforming encounter with God which brings:
  - a greater confidence in God's alongsideness in daily life;
  - a greater sense of being at home in the world;
  - a greater commitment to 'moral' behaviour.
- Religious experience is often triggered by the anxiety associated with being overwhelmed (through sickness or a crisis of some kind).[30]
- The vocational domain is likewise about risking or even practising being overwhelmed.

The vocational domain, in expressing fraternal commitment to those who know deeply about struggle, opens us to the possibility of being overwhelmed. Being without power when alongside those who know deeply about struggle can be distressing and even harrowing. It involves the risk of being overwhelmed, even though only through empathy. For there are no limits to the distress and suffering one might discover. The fact of not being in control can be an assault on our usual capacities and coping techniques and with this we open ourselves to the possibility – and even likelihood – of religious experience.

This equation is compelling, but more than this it is *precisely* what the market is seeking. The readiness of people to embrace the vocational domain with its potential for transformation is upon us. We have before us a hugely significant opportunity to promote the processes that Jesus commends, to enable people to sense God's presence and to partake of the transformational experiences that people want so much.

Notes

1 Zygmunt Bauman, *Life in Fragments* (Oxford: Blackwell, 1995), p. 37.
2 Ibid., p. 43.
3 Ibid., p. 264.
4 Rebecca Anne Allahyari, *Visions of Charity* (California: University of California Press, 2000), p. 4.
5 See Emmanuel Lévinas (1987) *Collected Philosophical Papers* (The Hague: Martinus Nijhoff, 1987), in particular 'Freedom and Command'.
6 With this encounter, each of us has three options: indifference; a state of openness and open-handedness which allows the encounter to continue or a conventional or stereo-typical response.
7 Hans Jonas, *Philosophical Essays: from Ancient Creed to Technological Man* (Englewood Cliffs: Prentice Hall, 1974), p. 19, quoted in Bauman, op. cit.
8 Parker J. Palmer, (1983) *To Know as We Are Known* (San Francisco: Harper Row, 1983), p. 47.
9 Ibid., p. 49.
10 Ibid., pp. 53–4.
11 Ibid., p. 56.
12 James Alison, *Faith Beyond Resentment* (London: Darton, Longman and Todd, 2001) p. 74.
13 Martin Buber, *I and Thou*, translated with prologue and notes by Walter Kaufmann, (Edinburgh: T & T Clark, 1970).
14 Karl W. Deutsch, *The Nerves of Government* (London and New York: Free Press of Glencoe, 1963), p. 230.
15 Richard Sennett, (2003) *Respect* (London: Allen Lane, 2003), p. 20.
16 Ibid., p. 177.
17 Mary Douglas in the foreword to Marcel Mauss, *The Gift*, trans. W. D. Halls (London: Routledge, 1990), p. xvi. This reference is taken from Richard Sennet (2003), op.cit., p. 219.

18 Hannah Arendt, (1996) *Love and St Augustine*, eds and trans. Joanna Vecchiarelli Scott and Judith Chelius Stark (Chicago: University of Chicago Press, 1996), p. 97, cited by Sennett, op. cit., p. 139.

19 Stanley Saunders and Charles Campbell, *The Word on the Street* (Grand Rapids, Michigan: Eidmans, 2000). pp. 2–3.

20 B. Joseph Pine and James H Gilmore (1999) *The Experience Economy* (Boston, Mass.: Harvard Business School Press, 1999), p. 165.

21 Virginia I. Postrel, 'It's All in the Head', *Forbes ASAP*, 26 February 1996: 118 (reference from Pine and Gilmore, note p. 228).

22 Pine and Gilmore, op. cit., p. 180.

23 Ibid., p. 178.

24 Ibid., p. 178.

25 More simply put, Camden is a trendy place with lots of different styles, visit Camden Lock, see and be seen ... and spend!

26 Pine and Gilmore, op. cit., p. 165.

27 Ibid., p. 182.

28 Ibid., p. 190.

29 Richard Sennet, op. cit, p. 56.

30 See chapter 8 for a fuller discussion of the triggers and outcomes of religious experience.

A Coda[1]

When the Wine Runs Out

I love the story of Jesus and his mates at the wedding of someone his mother knew.[2] It is this story that has been in my mind and in my heart whilst writing this book so it is fitting that it should be the basis for my concluding comments. I can't help but smile that a wedding where the wine was running out should provide the setting for the first explicit sign that Jesus is the Son of God. I like to ponder what kind of internal conversation Jesus must have had with Himself when nudged into action by His mother. One can only assume that it came as some surprise to Him that His *outing* should be associated with such an earthy and apparently irreligious challenge.

This first miracle, where Jesus stepped into the breach when the booze was running out, I find a wonderful allegory for our plight today. Surely, in our parlous state as churches we must fear that the wine has run out. Surely we too experience that mixture of disappointment, embarrassment and anxiety associated with running out of steam, running out of wine or just running out. The allegory for our current plight continues, for it involves action by others, especially the already weary servants, who are required to draw gallons and gallons of water from the well in order to fill the jars. Their internal as well as spoken conversations must have been quite choice. How they found the motivation to follow such bizarre instructions God alone knows. Then, of course, the miracle itself is so bizarre; high-quality wine, about 130 gallons of the stuff, begins to flow to add to the delight of the celebration – which had already been in full swing for three days. No wonder Jesus resisted the idea that such would be the occasion when His time had come. Please God may this also be an allegory for the renewal of the Church.

I understand that Alcoholics Anonymous in Britain is run by only three paid staff based in York. There may be as many AA branches in each town in Britain as there are churches. Furthermore, there may be as many people who come to an active faith and relationship with God as a result of AA, who do so as a result of the ministrations of the churches. In fact, it could be argued that Alcoholics Anonymous is the church we do not know we have. It is a mixed blessing indeed that AA goes from strength to strength, but nevertheless, there may be a lot for us to learn from AA.[3]

Unlike AA, statistics show that Church membership continues to decline. Clearly the extensive secular and materialistic culture that prevails and the loss of interest in corporate or community activities have contributed to this. Today, led by the media, churches are considered to be irrelevant or outmoded, and even a dangerous *hangover* from medieval times. Our current situation is so different from the past centuries which shaped our Church habits, we should not be surprised that our churches creak and even crumble. The wine has run out and the party seems to be drawing to a close.

The situation that we face today is novel. We cannot rely on previous habits and structures to help us cope, let alone flourish in such unfamiliar terrain. The challenge of responding prophetically and creatively to this new context belongs not just to church leaders, it is also a challenge for the million or more regular churchgoers who invest time and money in the current ways of being church. The fact that our churches need to change has certainly percolated into our consciousness. However, the dominant inclination is to endeavour to maintain the established features of church life, but to do so on a shoestring. The immediate and common-sense way of coping with ever-declining resources is for lay people to take responsibility for more and more aspects of church life. This is commendable on one level, but it is an inherently conservative approach. This development does not begin to take seriously the huge, complex and non-negotiable changes that have come upon us at all levels of society. We must be careful therefore to ensure that lay leadership, in the context of ever-diminishing resources, does not equate to taking responsibility for more and more jobs *in* church. People's participation and commitment is a priceless resource, and should not be constrained or, dare I say, domesticated by the implicit expectation that ultimately it must serve the Church, rather than journey out and embrace a struggle for the peaceful, shalom future of God's creation.

The hangover that the Church is still recovering from results from having imbibed the potent liquor served by the powerful of the nation. A millennium of carousing with kings, queens and ministers of state takes its toll. This seat at the top table was ensured by the Church's capacity for social control. Now the magic or, at least, the threat of eternal damnation no longer convinces. The Church has been cast off, rejected by the powerful; the courtship has ended. However, the legacy is the unacknowledged habit of investing huge amounts of time, effort and money in policing orthodoxy. The need to ensure everyone is doing things by the book (and I'm not referring to the Bible here) is a neurosis that plagues us from days gone by, when the Church was an agent of social control for the maintenance of Christendom. It is a tough inheritance to unpick and from which to free ourselves.

Once again Alcoholics Anonymous could show us a way of acknowledging and freeing ourselves from the inebriate supping with power. AA can do no other than trust people who are fragile and vulnerable. Each AA branch is run by people who have come to know their vulnerability, who know what it is like to risk being overwhelmed each and every day. The Church so far, has yet to learn how to trust the broken and beaten-down. Yet Jesus repeatedly urges us to do something as bizarre as this. The Church has yet to admit that it is vulnerable and broken down. Furthermore, the Church has to face up to the possibility that it too could be in a process of being overwhelmed and, like the chronic alcoholic, will have to confess that its life has become unmanageable.

The first of the twelve steps that AA urges upon the alcoholic is to admit that his or her life is unmanageable. The alcoholic then faces other challenges:

◆ to believe that 'God as we understand Him can restore us to sanity';

◆ to 'Make a decision to turn our will and our lives over to the care of God';

◆ to 'Make a searching and fearless moral inventory of ourselves';

◆ to 'Pray to God to remove defects of character';

◆ to 'Endeavour to make amends to those whom one has harmed';

◆ to 'Make a commitment to meditation and prayer and a commitment to carry the message of the possibility of freedom from alcoholism to others whose lives are dominated by alcohol.'[4]

I am struck by how the route that has to be followed by the alcoholic provides an extraordinarily apt map for the established Churches to follow. The challenge to those of us who are committed to the Church is whether we can marshal the same honesty, commitment to struggle and faith in God as the alcoholics who meet together at AA meetings.

Bosch, in his masterly book *Transforming Mission*,[5] traces the different approaches to mission adopted in different era. He examines the understanding of mission held by each of the Gospel writers and then by Paul, the most self-conscious of missioners in the early Church. He then goes on to explore the practice and model of mission in the wake of the

Enlightenment and during the last century. Bosch's work illustrates the paradigm shifts that have occurred in the way in which mission has been understood and carried out through the history of the Church worldwide. His detailed scholarship makes it clear that 'At no time in the past two millennia was there a single "theology of mission"'.[6] This straightforward insight is worth taking to heart for it encourages us to recognize that church life and practice do not have to be like it this, church life could be different. This, of course, is the first message that the alcoholic has to accept: that life could be different.

My case is that when we journey out, without power, aware of our vulnerability and all the time risking that we may be overwhelmed, we will find ourselves being church and doing holistic mission à la Bosch, and we will be able to serve up the finest quality wine in extravagant amounts. Like the weary and drunken servants at the wedding celebration we have to find a way of trusting the promise of a cascade of grace that will follow when we are prepared to do what Jesus tells us. Do we, like those at the wedding celebration at Cana, have the energy and willingness to do something quite different, to do something that will demand effort, but not effort in obvious directions?

The Church, like the chronic alcoholic, has to go through a process of detox, clearing out from the system the toxins that would otherwise bring death. Power has been the poison that has prevented the institutional Church from understanding the Gospel. Now shorn of power it is not just a case of the Church understanding the Gospel afresh, but of understanding for the first time. This freedom to see the radicalness of the Gospels has come with the end of Christendom. Ever since the first time the Emperor Constantine identified with the Christian faith and promoted it across the Roman Empire the institutional Church has never been vulnerable and without power. Now we have no option but to accept our vulnerability and the possibility of being overwhelmed.

When the Church understands the Gospel in its fullness, it

takes seriously not just the death and resurrection of Jesus, but His life too, and in taking the life of Jesus seriously, we gain new tools and new approaches for living. Kingdom reversals cease to be just part of Jesus' miraculous gifting and become practical and available to us today. It means we can see that the place of vulnerability, and being without power, is a place which enables us to be effective, because at this point we become open-handed, ready and welcoming to receive anything which comes to our aid, including the Holy Spirit. It is when we are stripped of our power that we discover a deep spirituality. This spirituality is produced obliquely; it is an emergent property that results from being in the right place, having journeyed out to embrace fraternal relations with the stranger despite our vulnerability and powerlessness.

It is only now that we have the capacity to see the coherence and potential viability of the processes that Jesus commends to us. These processes turn on their head the accepted or common-sense assumptions that prevail in the wider world. In order to embrace holistic ministry, it is not just a case of believing that salvation comes through faith in Jesus. Faith is also needed in relation to the processes that Jesus demonstrated and commended. Now, like the alcoholic, the Church has to face up to the fact that its life is unmanageable and take steps to reorder every aspect of its life. Just as AA offers the alcoholic twelve steps to recovery, so too Jesus has demonstrated and urged us to follow distinctive processes or steps that will enable our life to be different, and to be a life with fullness beyond anything we can contemplate.

Step 1   Practise seeing the world from the perspectives of those who are most excluded.

Step 2   Avoid resentment and 'tit-for-tat' behaviour – just as Jesus demonstrated.

Step 3 Embrace fraternal relations beyond our earthly family.[7]

Step 4 The Christian way of knowing is via relationship.

Step 5 Prayer makes a difference, we cannot afford not to do it.

Step 6 Acknowledge weakness and vulnerability, trusting that they provide a robust foundation on which to cooperate and work for the Kingdom of God.

Step 7 Resist the rush to possess truth, or we will find that we risk some snake telling us what to think and do.

Step 8 Accept the challenge of journeying out, with concern for the world rather than for ourselves, 'For whoever finds his life will lose it, and whoever loses his life for my sake will find it'.[8]

The Church has to decide whether it can put its faith in the steps or processes that Jesus taught us. If the Church can face the reality of its broken state and Jesus' offer of a way through, then the Church can become very different to the Church with which we are familiar. Church becomes a place where people can practise and rehearse these steps which Jesus has shown us, and in doing so we will find ourselves party to an extraordinary cascade of grace. And as any recovered alcoholic will testify, it is essential to say these things to ourselves – and to others – even if we cannot yet do them. This is a measure of God's graceful economy.

Notes

1 Coda: a passage added after the natural completion of a movement, so as to form a more definite and satisfactory conclusion – see how my knowledge of classical music has progressed!
2 John 2.1-11.

3 The scope for churches to learn from Alcoholics Anonymous was first identified by C. Hobart Mowbray in his book *The Crisis in Psychiatry and Religion* (New York: Van Nostrand, 1961), p. 46. Claire Dalpras has followed up this insight in 'Addicted to Planting?', '*Encounters on the Edge*' No. 17 published by the Church Army, The Sheffield Centre, 50 Cavendish Street, Sheffield S3 7RZ.

4 Taken from *The Twelve Steps and Twelve Traditions* produced by AA General Service Office, PO Box 1, Stonebow House, Stonebow, York YO1 2NJ.

5 David J. Bosch, *Transforming Mission* (New York: Orbis, 1991).

6 Ibid., p. 8.

7 Don't act bemused by Jesus repeatedly refusing to acknowledge the prior claim upon Him from His mother and His brothers. Jesus makes the point very clearly to us that in sharing a Heavenly Father we have a limitless vista of brothers and sisters.

8 Matthew 10.39.

Glossary

Adaequatio: Thomas Aquinas maintained that a person needs to have some inner capacity to receive what is to be known if knowledge is to result from the encounter.

Adaptive zone: A term that is used in evolutionary biology to describe a period in which a number of environmental factors work together to facilitate a leap in the evolution of a species.

Apt liturgy: A specific liturgy which aims at including people with little faith and Christian knowledge and often focuses on a particular distress that has arisen within a community.

Bonding social capital: Strong allegiance between people that can carry support, but can lead to resentment in those who perceive themselves as excluded.

Brave social capital: Willingness to provide support to those who are likely to be perceived as carrying some kind of threat or menace.

Bridging social capital: Willingness to extend support to those beyond one's interest group, i.e. including the stranger.

Capacity building: Training and coaching key members of a community to enable them to exercise leadership in relation to public services and community action.

Cascade of grace: The generous outpouring of positive outcomes, many of which are unanticipated and contribute to a virtuous circle.

Christendom: That extensive period in history when the Christian faith dominated all levels of society and when people would have had familiarity with the tenets of the Christian faith and assumed that the Christian belief equated to reality.

Epistemology: Ways of knowing or achieving knowledge.

Experience economy: The latest type of economic output – creating and selling experiences.

Explicit domain: Where explicit Christian teaching is provided, but also carries the overlay of each denomination or church culture.

Foundational domain: The work that the Church now has to do to help people gain confidence in their perception or intimation of there being an enduring reality and the possibility of God.

Fraternal relations: The all-embracing relationship which enables us to call everyone our brother or sister because we share the same Heavenly Father.

Generative stories: Stories in our lives that have an emotional potency and carry an imperative to action.

Gospel or Kingdom reversals: The teaching and life of Jesus demonstrate the viability of values and practices that turn upside down the values and habits that are taken for granted in the wider world. This reversal of worldly assumptions and practices is the basis of the term 'up-side-down Kingdom' being used to describe the new reality that Jesus proclaims and demonstrates.

Hegemony: Sometimes referred to as engineered consensus, the ability to disguise the pattern of benefits associated with the *status quo*.

High symbols: These allude to the sacred and signify those aspects of life that can only be partly known.

Holistic mission: A term coined by David Bosch to describe the importance of achieving both work for the Kingdom of God and the proclamation of Jesus as Saviour.

Individuation: A term from depth psychology which describes the formation of a robust identity that can withstand the shaping forces of the wider environment and enables the person to separate from the crowd and stick their neck out.

Iron cage of bureaucracy: A term coined by Max Weber to describe the problem that is caused when rational thinking is applied extensively, leading to systematized responses that inhibit flexibility and spontaneity and result in defensive bureaucracies.

Moral-selving: A term used by Allahyari to describe the gathering of moral ideas and endeavouring to act upon them.

Needs-meeting philosophy: A perspective that assumes that by providing services to meet people's needs progress will be made, based on the liberal premise that progress comes through the application of reason and rationality.

Neighbourhood renewal: A Government initiative in relation to the 10 per cent poorest wards in England which emphasizes the involvement of local people in prioritizing issues and, ideally, being involved in the response.

Opportunity cost: An economic concept that emphasizes the cost incurred in doing one thing rather another, i.e. we have to take into account the value of the opportunities that have be forgone.

Plausibility structures: The ideas and opinions that support, or make believable (plausible), a particular world view or ideology.

Praxis: The commitment to action and reflecting on that action in order to learn from experience.

Principle of obliquity: The notion that in complex situations pursuing an objective head-on may work against the achievement of that object, instead an indirect or 'oblique' approach is required.

Relational consciousness: Nye has coined this expression to describe this increased attentiveness to the well-being of others, and even to the world itself, that seems to be linked with the growth of spiritual awareness and religious experience.

Social capital: The level of reciprocal relationships and trustworthy networks that exist within a locality or society.

Social Gospel: The idea that social progress provides a significant route towards the Kingdom of God.

Swarming: A term used by biologists and borrowed by economists to describe how species, and organizations, can rush to take advantage of certain conditions (an adaptive zone or an innovation in technology) without being fully equipped to deal with the apparently favourable environment.

Symbolic interactionism: A perspective used in anthropology and sociology which focuses on how communication between people relies on a willingness to share the same symbols or negotiate a shared understanding of their signicance.

Telos: A Greek word meaning the deep purpose of life or existence.

Theory of action (or **theory of mission**): The strategy one adopts based on one's assessment of what factors have to be taken into account if one is to achieve one's purpose.

Thin place: An expression used by George MacLeod to describe Iona - a place where only a tissue separates us from a sense of God's presence. There are other contexts and situations that may have a similar quality.

Vocational domain: The opportunity provided to enable people to respond to that sense within them that they could do more in their lives in relation to risk and concern for others.

INDEX

Words that are included in the glossary on pages 237-41 are indicated in bold

vulnerable, vulnerability vii, 1, 97,
    111, 112, 113, 114, 160, 172,
    174, 190, 195, 196, 209, 212,
    215, 231-2, 233, 234, 235

Wallis, Jim 8
Walsh, Margaret 60
wealthy 37
Weber, Max 30, 31
wedding at Cana 41, 229-30, 233
wellbeing 96
welfare,
    dependence on 51
    provision 53
Williams, Raymond 120

Wilson, William Julius 50
winter nightshelters 11-13, 28, 37,
    61, 71-2, 104
    assessing outcomes of 29, 32
women 53, 62, 68, 75, 92n, 122,
    131
    older women 65n, 67, 75, 136n
    Syro-Phoenician 132-3, 134, 135
worship 146, 157, 183
wounded history (*see* also
    memories) 162, 164, 180n

Yom Kippur 163

Zimbabwe 62, 67, 73